The Handbook of Home Design

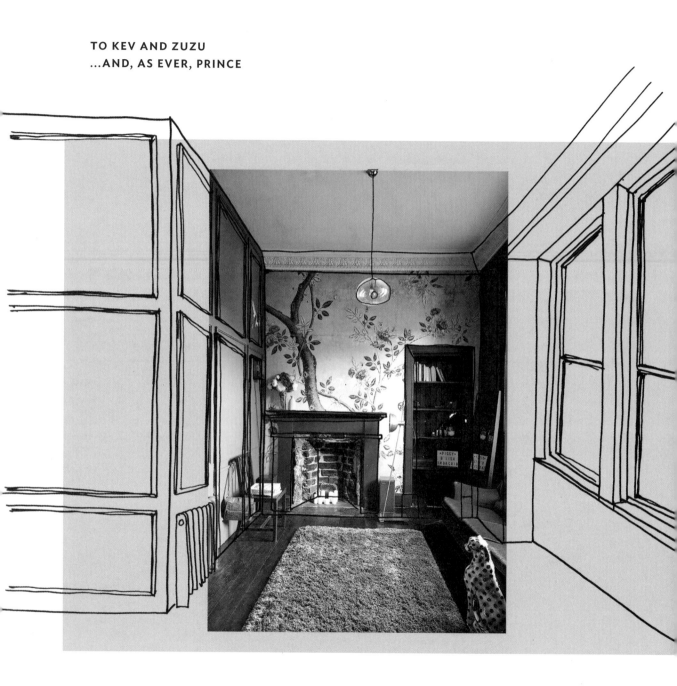

KYLE BOOKS

The Handbook of Home Design

AN ARCHITECT'S BLUEPRINT
FOR SHAPING YOUR HOME

Laura Jane Clark

Contents

Introduction

There has never been so much demand for a better way of living, for ownership of our own homes and style or access to such a wealth of design and building techniques. But when the people who occupy a home come to renovate or extend it, the design process is often taken out of their hands. They are asked 'what do you want?', but the solution is presented as a large box of an extension with a couple of odd skylights thrown in if they are lucky. I know I am being facetious here, but I am certainly not exaggerating the experiences recounted to me by countless homeowners over the last decade.

The time for change is now. I want homeowners to have some control; a say in what they want and how they want to live, and for their homes to reflect that. It is a cliché to say that our homes are our sanctuary, but if every day you have to fight to find your coat, or are unable to eat in the room that you want to, or to cook dinner because you need to finish the laundry first, then we are not winning. Our homes aren't working for us – they are working against us.

This 'architect's approach' to home design seeks to give you the responses to the fundamental issues that I come across over and over again in houses and flats around the country. I have over 15 years' experience as a qualified architect redesigning, extending and building homes. This book uses a step-by-step approach to show you how I approach a new design and give you the confidence, language and ability to communicate your vision. It will also give you architectural insight, ideas and inspiration, allowing you to be in control and become the most important part of the creative process and the build. It is your home after all.

This is my personal guide, written as if I am there with you. It covers everything from how to read a plan, to identifying problem areas and pinch points, to showing you how I approach design. It looks at all the questions and discussions you should have with your design team and builder to ensure you get the most out of your design, and ultimately love your finished home.

Going deeper than a simple room-by-room design guide, it looks at the house holistically. Once you have discovered the fundamentals of how to read a plan and create a project brief, it moves on to the design concepts that will help you achieve your dreams seamlessly.

This handbook will not only give you the inspiration and motivation, but also the confidence to tackle a building project from that initial spark of an idea to the finished build. Whether you are looking to extend, reconfigure or rebuild; if your budget is £1,500 ($1,726) or £350,000 ($402,721); you are experienced in home renovation or this is your first project, this book is a unique and an invaluable source of design ideas and practical advice, and I will be with you every step of the way. By giving you a deep insight into my thought process, *The Handbook of Home Design* seeks to democratize the concept of residential architectural design.

Homeowners rarely feel engaged in the minutiae of laying out their own home. Historically, a house or flat is somewhere you moved into, only really having ownership over the paint colours and soft furnishings. Very occasionally, when buying new builds off-plan, you might have the opportunity to 'upgrade' the fittings such as kitchen worktops, just like when buying a new car, but that is as far as it goes.

Unpicking the past, the history of our homes, gives us an insight into why we are where we are. Why aren't cultural and societal shifts reflected in our homes? They can be seen in our choice of décor, but not in the skeleton of residential architecture. For most people, storage and utility rooms are a luxury, but for me they are the building blocks of the home. Why, from the 19th right up until the mid-20th centuries, were kitchens so cramped and tiny? When did the kitchen hatch come into common use, and what has become of it? Why do we keep our washing machines in the kitchen? Why have we reverted from the utopian designs

of the 1960s and 1970s with open-plan living and large picture windows, to mock Tudor and faux Georgian new-build homes? These questions run around my head like an earworm, and I get frustrated seeing the same fundamental problems repeated in both new-build homes, renovations, refurbishments and extensions.

Being able to see your home in terms of the era it was built, its story and development, allows you to see the opportunities it holds, as well as the limitations and parameters you need to work within. No Victorian terraced house is the same, it won't even be identical to its neighbour. Our homes have been measured and built by hand and cannot be perfectly replicated. This isn't a one-size-fits-all approach to design, but there are similar themes when approaching a 1940s, post-war house opposed to a flat in an Edwardian terrace.

Once you have explored and touched every wall of every room, you can get started on the fun part! I will go through how to draw up your space and establish what you want and need from your home. Together, we will then build on these fundamental elements for your first dip into home design. Your first thought is never the final design, so we will look at ways to conquer the fear of the blank page and

getting pen to paper. Step-by-step, with achievable aspirational ideas, insight and inspiration, we will bring your sketch ideas to fruition in your home.

My office floor is often strewn with sheets of tracing paper covered in drawings and ideas, some good and some very bad. (It has not been unknown for me to wrap gifts in my old unused drawings, I am all about reusing here.) It can be quite daunting to start to put any newly acquired skill into practice. I think there is a common misconception that design is always right the first time, and mistakes are rarely made. When walking around a friend's house, I am often asked: 'so what would you do with this?' My honest answer? 'I haven't a clue.' It takes me hours of sketching different ideas, drawing sightlines and the path of the sun, and imagining walking around the space to get to the point where I can finalize a layout. It can take anywhere from three hours to three days, and I have been doing it for over 20 years since studying at architecture school.

I try to achieve simplicity in my designs. The concept of making design look effortless, so that it works so well you can't understand why it wasn't always like this, is key for me. But don't think that creating a design that is this simple and effortless must be easy – nothing could be further from the truth. I go by the age-old adage of the grace and beauty of a swan gliding on the water, while there is the mad frantic paddling underneath the surface. And maybe that is the reason why architects and designers don't really want to share their ideas? In university, student architects are pitted against one another, with their tutors using long words that I always had to look up. It was instilled in us from day one that the very thought of us ending up with a career designing kitchen extensions would equate to abject failure as an architect. It has taken me years to come to terms with the fact that this is way off the mark.

But I think this contributes to the reason why so many of our homes are, and continue to be, so badly designed. Architects who are trained in turning thoughts and needs into designs don't work on standard residential projects, and architectural technicians tend not to have the training, yet they appear to be the ones working in most of this country's homes. I want this book to bridge that gap so that when you are asked 'what do you want me to do?', you will be able to confidently deliver a scaled hand-sketched concept design that you have spent time on and that illustrates what you want to build and, more importantly, how you want to live.

Instead of jumping with talk of pocket doors and chevron flooring, I have written these chapters to give you a solid foundation you can build upon.

AN UNDERSTANDING OF THE AGE AND HERITAGE OF YOUR HOME WILL HELP YOU TO INTEGRATE CONTEMPORARY DESIGN IDEAS WITHOUT CREATING A PASTICHE OR AN AWKWARD CLASH OF STYLES.

A bit like gardening, you can't just grab a few growbags and a packet of seeds and expect to be self-sufficient in a couple of weeks. Ironically, though, that was my first approach to starting a veg patch a few years ago. Needless to say it failed. Badly. I want to demystify the process of architectural design and in doing so, give you the opportunity for real and positive change in your home; a change that you are in control of.

Armed with both an in-depth and unique knowledge of your home and your drawing skills, you can start to explore the design ideas and proposals that are essentially the translation of your brief and the fabric of your existing property into a home that is tailor-made for you.

So let's take the first step: come with me on this home design odyssey.

LOOKING STRAIGHT THROUGH THIS BROKEN-PLAN GROUND FLOOR YOU CAN SEE HOW THE SEATING ZONE IS TUCKED AWAY FROM THE KITCHEN AND DINING AREA AND HIGHLIGHTED BY THE ROOF GLAZING. THE BRICKWORK, BLACK STEEL-FRAMED DOORS AND BRASS IRONMONGERY GIVE AN ELEGANT BACKDROP TO THIS FAMILY HOME.

History of the home

How on earth did we get here?

'Each house is linked by a covered passageway, with the individual homes made up of one large living space with a floor of stone slabs. Around a central hearth is a fitted dresser and two bed pods with storage tanks sunk into the ground.'

This quote on the left may sound like a description of a progressive 21st-century communal housing development, but in fact this is a description of Skara Brae, a Neolithic settlement built some 5,000 years ago that still survives to this day on Orkney to the north of Scotland.

I know that I won't need any evidence to back up my argument that the concept of 'home' is not a brand-new invention. We have been living in some form of built shelter for millennia. Yet I find it staggering that so little thought has gone into the layout of our houses and flats, how after all these years we still can't seem to get it right. Time and time again I am given house plans that either make no logical sense, or do not work for the family for which they were intended. I visit homes both large and small that have very little natural light, are dark and cramped, without flow and my personal cardinal sin: zero storage. More often than not, I am told that the homeowner isn't happy with their plans but felt that they couldn't explain why it doesn't work to the architect or builder, either because they can't quite find the language to explain why they aren't happy, or they don't have the confidence to argue their point of view.

Poor housing stock can't be excused because it is simply easier for a builder to construct a square extension with endless corridors, or a developer choosing to maximize profit over the creation of a flowing family home. To understand how we have got to this, we need to understand where we have come from.

This chapter is not a rehashing of our existing architectural history, but a narrative exploration drawing on our social history, technological advances, immigration, emigration, cultural shifts, where we have succeeded and where, as a society, we have failed. I will share my thoughts on how on earth we have got to a point in the 21st century where our kitchens are too small, our bathrooms too cramped and we are still drying our trousers on radiators.

The past,
the present
+ the future

Like fashion, architecture and design are constantly evolving and taking inspiration from the world around them, whether that is the present day, history or fantasy. The concept that the length of skirt hemlines is directly linked to the economy is well-known, with the mini being mainstream fashion in times of prosperity, and maxi dresses appearing in times of recession. We are used to being able to express ourselves through quickly changing and affordable fashion, yet it has only been in the last 20 years or so that we have had the equivalent choice in how we decorate and furnish our homes. Now we can embrace and revel in styles of interior decoration like never before, yet the majority of new homes are still based on centuries-old designs. Why is this?

Let's take a step back in time. In the 19th century, the British population expanded from roughly 11 million to 32 million people. Catalyzed by the Industrial Revolution, the 2 million residents of our cities boomed to 20 million. Workers lived in high density, poor housing with little or no sanitation or fresh water. Overcrowded, disease-ridden, urban slums were synonymous with the huge powerhouse industrial and ship-building cities of the north, as well as London, Birmingham and Glasgow. On the flipside, there were

not only individual fortunes to be made from manufacturing and trading, but also huge swathes of employment opportunities for skilled labour, technical and clerical roles. Men – it was undoubtedly mainly men – were now defined by their job rather than their background. The expansion of the railway network in the Victorian era increased the mobility of both this new, burgeoning middle class and also the transportation of materials and goods around the country. In the late Victorian and early Edwardian period, new villas and large detached houses were built for these upwardly mobile families. For those of more modest means, terraced and smaller, semi-detached houses were built in great numbers, creating suburbs with ostentatious, classical details as an outward show of wealth, maybe to separate themselves absolutely and visually from the poor, renting, working class that they, their parents or grandparents, were once a part of.

It is commonplace for architectural history to focus on the development of housing built for the increasingly rich middle classes. But by 1914 these owner-occupied homes made up only 10 per cent of properties in England. The remaining 90 per cent were the rented homes of factory and mill workers, colliers and miners, immigrants fleeing persecution and people from nations where the labour of previous generations had supplied the cotton that fuelled the mills and made the sugar that fed rich and – increasingly – poor

alike. Although over the centuries there were many movements to improve living conditions and provide sanitation for all, generally, mass housing was cheaply built and of extremely high density, with back-to-back terraces and tenement flats often creating contained courtyards with communal latrines and wash houses. I can't possibly begin to imagine the deprivation suffered by the people who lived in these overcrowded slums, yet I wonder whether a deep sense of community was forged through adversity and proximity. Maybe a gritty, generations-deep sense of pride of place that you don't get in, say, Sevenoaks or Welwyn Garden City.

Mining towns such as Ferndale in the Rhondda valley, South Wales, built hierarchy into mine workers' homes. Set on a steep hillside, the terraced homes that housed the general pit workers had a front door that opened straight onto the street. Several streets up, the terraces of the more skilled workers were set back slightly from the pavement. And yet further up the hill, the pit managers enjoyed a small front garden and their homes looked down over the valley. In order to move into those larger, more gentrified houses, those working at the coalface knew that all they had to do was work. Hard.

Home as a marker of status and personal achievement is deeply rooted in our collective psyche. Those in the working classes who possessed the skills that allowed them to follow a career leading to personal wealth, be it small or large, were afforded options, mobility and, crucially, homeownership. The ability to own your own home is one of the reasons that boundary disputes and quarrels between neighbours are so common.

After World War I, there was a renewed push for new homes. Inspiration came from housing associations and wealthy, philanthropic factory owners such as the Cadbury family, who built the village of Bournville for workers at its chocolate factory outside Birmingham at the end of the 19th century. These businessmen wanted to house their workers in sanitary conditions, with a focus on outdoor green space and the occupants' health.

Nationwide, the semi-detached model became fairly standard, each house had a garden in which to grow fruit and vegetables, and they were built on estates with tree-lined roads. The bungalow appeared and gained swift popularity, particularly in coastal towns.

The style of these homes rejected the monotonous Victorian terrace and reflected a quainter Arts and Crafts sentiment with mock-Tudor half-timbered detailing and leaded windows, despite the advances in glazing that had been made in the decades before. These new semi-detached homes typically had three bedrooms, with a small kitchen, living and dining rooms, and a bathroom with a separate toilet. Homeownership boomed and, between the wars, a divide in house building began. New homes were either built well, providing excellent value with high-quality fixtures and fittings, or were quickly constructed by unscrupulous builders with features such as large windows and chimney breasts removed to save money.

Following World War II, when nearly half a million homes were destroyed but many urban slums were still occupied, rebuilding plans were revived. Advances in materials and technology, such as concrete and

prefabrication, came into their own, and new 'temporary' houses were built. Some of these homes, that were intended to have a lifespan of 20 years, are still with us today. With the exponential increase in house building – homeownership reached just below 40 per cent in the middle of the 20th century – came the rise in profits of builders and developers. With it came the push for homes and furniture, bathroom suites and kitchen appliances, as a lifestyle statement. We had entered the era of the home as a status symbol for all. Well, nearly all.

The space race and the moon landing in the mid-20th century gave rise to an obsession with the future. In this 'future' everyone wore insulated silver space coats, and kids on hover boards were a menace on the spotless streets. Home design also embraced the wonder and inspiration of films such as Stanley Kubrick's *2001: A Space Odyssey*, the James Bond 'Space One' (the actual title *Moonraker* always eludes me) and the beautiful set

designs of Ken Adam and Rick Carter.

In the early 1960s, the average British housewife completed about 70 hours of housework a week, as a result the market for household goods was vast. Inventions such as the automated washing machine, microwave, bedside Teasmade and the electric toaster and egg poacher came thick and fast. Some, understandably, didn't stand the test of time.

Were these gadgets designed to give more time for the woman of the house to relax, further educate herself or start her own career? I am not convinced, but it did mean they could now clean quicker, cook more and have more children. We have retained many of these inventions from the last century, but our homes were not designed to accommodate them. The time-saving inventions of old have been overtaken by the space-saving inventions of today.

The mid-20th century was a time of huge innovation and the opening up of our world like never before.

For me, home design started to get really interesting in the 1960s and 1970s as it was a time of great innovation. Councils invested in mass housing, and architects and designers saw creating places for people to live as both a valuable commodity and a sound moral and economic decision. Despite this progress, the struggle for equality in society was being fought all over the world. Local authorities blazed a trail in residential architecture. At this time, when progressive, forward-thinking housing estates were being built, it was considered honourable for a newly qualified architect to apply for a design role in the housing department of their local council.

At this time, the concept of the vertical city, created by the French architect Le Corbusier, was introduced in the UK. Homes were built in a tower that was part of a fully functioning town with shops, hair salons, nurseries, play areas and even a fantastic residents' swimming pool on

the roof. It was a wonderful concept in the temperate South of France. But when this model was adopted to create high-density housing in our cities, communal elements including the shops, the hairdressers, the entertainment and, of course, the rooftop swimming pool were removed to cut costs. Instead of an urban utopia, the reality was cheaply built residential tower blocks. The horizontal slums of previous decades were replaced by vertical ones.

Even with the best planning intentions, new town failures were not only due to economic reasons. Cumbernauld in Scotland was designed as a pedestrian paradise, removing the danger of road accidents by physically separating the cars from the residents. A great idea in theory, but in practice, the poorly lit walkways and pedestrian tunnels became inhospitable, with pedestrians preferring to take their chances on the pavement-free roads.

In the 1980s, UK Prime Minister

Margaret Thatcher championed individualism. The butterfly effect of Right to Buy (which enabled council tenants to buy their homes), and the reduction in the power given to local authorities, continues to be felt in our housing stock. We are stuck in a time loop with developers running the show, regurgitating decades-old floor plans but adding a couple of solar panels as a gesture toward sustainability. Joined-up thinking by developers, architects, landscape architects, town planners and builders is the way ahead to ensure residents are at the forefront of design. Each member of the team must ask themselves: 'Would I like to live here?' The design and build of new homes must not be compromised by developers seeking solely to maximize profits. With democratic design at its heart, progressive models of housing can be created that are not only truly sustainable and economically viable, but wonderful green places to live, allowing communities to thrive.

Historically homes were an ostentatious show of wealth, status and taste. Sadly, history is repeating itself with mini mansions on cookie-cutter estates, nearly 2 m-high wooden fences separating the minimum required outdoor space from your neighbour's castle. It is unusual to see sensitively designed communal spaces, homes designed to fit their surroundings and landscape, and that create privacy and a sense of ownership through careful and thoughtful design, rather than

expecting people to shut their blinds and tut through the fence at their neighbour's dog barking. Things have been changing, however, and we are starting to learn from our mistakes. The number of successful housing schemes designed from the occupants' point of view has been growing. Intelligently designed housing and council housing estates with both the individual and community at their heart are starting to win illustrious architectural awards once again.

The turn of the 21st century has seen exponential growth in the homes and interiors market. Once the province of the wealthy, interior design now feels accessible to all with inspiration and ideas freely shared from all corners of the world through magazines, social media and online. Programmes like BBC's *Changing Rooms* were once compulsive viewing thanks to the mixture of excitement and horror over the clashing colour schemes, theme-park-like interiors and the designers playing an overblown parody of themselves. Today, the overarching purpose of home makeover and interior design shows is for the viewer to be enthralled by the realistic and achievable ideas and inspiration. I think that the popularization of accessible design on television and the expansion of Ikea in our towns and cities in the early 2000s kick-started our desire, and indeed our ability, for self-expression in our own homes.

Over the last few years, I have seen a dramatic shift in pride and

focus away from the slick, expensive kitchen island with mood lighting and integrated coffee maker to excitement over the inner workings of a hidden larder. Now we show off our kitchen prowess, style and taste through the inside of a well-designed cupboard.

We have started to take more ownership over our homes, and once more it is time for architects, designers and house builders to see the honour in designing and building kitchen extensions with the care and thought that they deserve, collectively shedding the inherent shame that has been woven into the very fabric of architectural education.

Another consideration is that our homes must adapt to reflect an ageing population. Plus we are staying put for longer because moving home is becoming increasingly costly, and swathes of young people are unable to get on the housing ladder themselves due to sky-rocketing house prices and rent. The lack of new, affordable houses being built and the state of our existing housing stock is also a problem. Moreover, we have the pressing need to address all of these issues in a sustainable and environmentally conscious way.

Excellence in home design is slowly coming back into fashion, and it is time for our nation's house builders to catch up.

Understanding your home

How the home has changed

If you ask a child to draw a house, they will draw a big square with square windows arranged symmetrically around a rectangular door, with a triangle for a roof with a smoking chimney. This is quite recognisably a simplification of a classical villa, despite what type of building the young illustrator might actually reside in. Why is this house type so deeply inset into our collective psyche? How have our homes become such an overt expression of wealth and taste?

Humans have always required shelter. Historically, our homes were either places to survive in, with communal latrines and typhoid-ridden water stands or, if you were wealthy, a status symbol with servants to empty your chamber pots and arrange the food on your dining table. As society has developed over the centuries, the idea of our homes as status symbols has endured and intensified, but has this been to the detriment of the true development of our homes to reflect our day-to-day needs?

When you research the grand houses of the 17th and 18th centuries such as Blenheim Palace, Attingham Park and Castle Howard, their architectural merit is only described

in terms of the external view of the imposing palace from the perspective of the jaw-dropped visitor. You rarely read reviews extolling the virtues of how the light falls in the dinner hall just in time for tea, or how magnificent the early-morning sunlight is as it dapples the kitchen walls when the staff are preparing breakfast. The architecture is designed to inspire awe, not to marvel at the comfortable living quarters within. The ancient architectural language of classical columns, huge amphitheatres, public bathhouses, and enormous temples set in the heat of the Mediterranean sun was brought together and regurgitated to fit the grandest country houses in cold and rainy Britain. The practical considerations of this translation were deemed unimportant; it was all about the spectacle.

I like to imagine a history only documented from the servants' perspective; architectural merit not credited on form or aesthetics, but on how easy it was to transport hot food from the kitchens to the dining room. Picture one of the great palaces being described not in the proportions of its windows, but on its naturally lit service routes that negated the need for staff to carry candles to light the way, reducing the number of fires and burns caused by naked flames.

Perhaps by delving into the history of the evolution of our typical house types, we will be able to answer the

BUILT ON THE SITE OF THE RUINED HENDERSKELFE CASTLE, CASTLE HOWARD IS AN 18TH-CENTURY STATELY HOME IN NORTH YORKSHIRE DESIGNED BY SIR JOHN VANBRUGH.

question 'how did we get here?'. This entails not simply looking at historical references, but understanding why our homes are often split, extended or remodelled in lazy ways that don't enhance our living space or reflect contemporary life. Rather than only concentrating on Georgian, Victorian and mid-20th-century semi-detached houses, we should shift the focus to include the plans for bungalows, tenement layouts and flats to help everyone, on any budget, re-plan, extend or rebuild with confidence.

In the 1970s Britain was influenced by radical shifts in design from Europe and America. Architects started shunning the symmetrical, typical Victorian aesthetic and progressed to an asymmetrical style with large panoramic windows and openings, rather than the tall, slim casement and sash windows of the preceding centuries. Large swathes of homes were built in this new style, typically with brick column detailing, timber cladding and tile-hung panels, large windows and open-plan living. But rather than embracing this revolution in architectural design, it was rejected by the masses who were firmly entrenched in the Victorian aesthetic. I do not think Britain was ready for it.

How did the traditional William Morris-patterned swags and tails, the chunky velour three-piece suites and heavy wooden dining tables and chairs fit with these oversized windows and large open-plan spaces? The collective love for half-timbered houses, Georgian and Victorian elegance was, and still is, hard to shake. Heading into the late 20th century, even though

lifestyles and family units were beginning to change, in our homes we continued to romanticize defunct 19th-century styles with tiny galley kitchens with a washing machine crammed in; small, freezing-cold bathrooms plumbed into the old outhouse; and divided-off living rooms.

I think it is an amusing irony that if there was a change in our furniture habits when these house types were being built, the rejection of the new would have been less universal. Yet now, if you flick through any glossy contemporary architecture and interiors magazine, you can't go a few pages without seeing Ludwig Mies Van der Rohe's classic *Barcelona* chair and refurbished G Plan teak furniture. It has taken us over half a century and the creation of a certain flat-pack furniture company to catch up and embrace the 'new'. The further irony of William Morris wallpapers and textiles now being the very height of sophistication is not lost on me.

As touched on in the previous chapter, the 1980s saw a transition from focusing on the greater good of society to the success of the individual. This shift was mirrored in architecture. The acclaim once heaped

TENEMENT FLATS, TYPICALLY BUILT IN SCOTTISH TOWNS AND CITIES, CONTAIN MULTIPLE APARTMENTS ON EACH FLOOR WITH A SHARED, COMMUNAL FRONT ENTRANCE AND A SHARED GARDEN SPACE TO THE REAR.

on architects for innovative housing estates and home design was now lavished on the designers of phallic towers erected to serve banks and private financial institutions. I think this has had huge ramifications on the reputation and expectations of what a successful architect is.

When I sat down for my first lecture as a student at the Mackintosh School of Architecture in Glasgow, my mind buzzing with excitement for my life to come, I was in for a shock. The first thing we were told was, in no uncertain terms, that in our careers 'most of us would do nothing more than kitchen extensions'. Those words have stuck with me and many of the

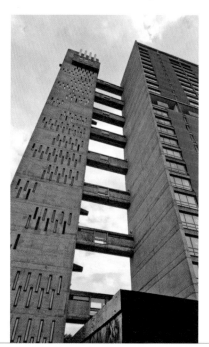

others I was with that morning. To add insult to injury, most of those students are now successful barristers, developers or schoolteachers, with only a handful of us admitting that we do indeed make our living from extending bathrooms. Instilling that sense of inadequacy and failure for a career in home design is something that has taken me decades to overcome. In fact, being candid, the reason that I am writing this book is symbolic of me finally accepting that what I am doing is architecturally worthwhile.

I find our collective lack of interest in the quality of our homes staggering. In 1967, when the Hungarian architect Ernö Goldfinger completed the Balfron Tower, a council-built housing scheme in London, he regarded his work so highly that he and his wife moved into an apartment on the 25th floor and held champagne gatherings so he could hear the residents' feedback to ensure the design of his next tower, the Trellick, would benefit from the experience of the occupants. A champagne lunch with your architect sounds rather bourgeois and pretentious, but he cared deeply about the affect of his architecture. I hope he provided the champagne himself.

As we hurtle toward the middle of the 21st century, how we use our homes has changed radically. With what seems to be an irrevocable move to part-time home working, there is a collective drive to increase the

THE BROWNFIELD ESTATE IN LONDON, FEATURING THE BALFRON TOWER, IS A BRUTALIST HOUSING ESTATE DESIGNED, AND LIVED IN, BY THE ARCHITECT ERNÖ GOLDFINGER.

THE HANDBOOK OF HOME DESIGN

quality of our housing stock as well as the physical and mental health of its residents. We are suddenly realizing how quickly and cheaply our homes have been altered and extended in piecemeal ways over the decades, with little or no thought to the effect on the overall house and, indeed, its occupants. Gaining space in the home was done as cheaply as possible as there was no economic justification for spending a huge amount of money on a bathroom extension. It was freezing cold and covered in mould, and that was just the way it was. I can see how this happened, but I struggle to accept that it must continue.

In the past, profit margins and house prices were so low relative to the average wage that, when extending, there was no time or budget to create flow and elegance, just speed and square footage. Nowadays, with the value of homes in most areas of Britain sky-rocketing, there are huge profits to be made from extending, altering and building new houses. Rather than apportioning some of that value to design, the higher profits are swallowed by developers who are still churning out cookie-cutter housing estates using decades-old house plans, their only real interest being their profit margin.

The value of homes couldn't be much different from 50 years ago, but our lack of investment in good design for all, is the same. Even brand-new housing developments have washing outside drying on racks and storage boxes crammed in at the windows. We do not seem to have learned anything.

As homeowners, we seem to be so removed from the design process, the ability to know what we want and how to get it from our homes. I see so many people experiencing a sense of shame about their homes, the untidiness or the feeling of separation and division within. Although good home design may not be the sole remedy for untidiness – sadly it hasn't lessened mine – it will bring light and flow to your floor plan and your lives too. It's time to banish any feelings of unease or misgivings you have about your home and get one step closer to creating the home of your dreams.

When you look closely at mid-20th-century housing estates and homes, it is rare that they retain any original features. More often than not, the flat planar roof sections have been replaced with twee pitched hips, and expanses of glass replaced with casement windows with fake lead diamond detailing in an attempt to 'Victorianize' the modern.

With any property, working with the design aesthetic rather than against it is key. Understanding the principal of the original architect's intention will allow you to create a template that you can work within. Emphasizing the linearity is a beautiful way to show the character of long, slender Victorian terraced houses, with pockets of light and width as you walk through the layout. Homes built in the 1960s had large wide windows and squarer, more open rooms. It is not about being slavish to the original design, or creating a pastiche, but reflecting elements such as the proportions of the spaces and impact of the glazing will give rise to a cohesive yet

EVEN IN FLATS THAT ARE BEING ERECTED TODAY, THERE ARE OFTEN CLEAR SIGNS THAT THERE IS NOT ENOUGH STORAGE OR PROVISION FOR LAUNDRY, WITH CLOTHES AIRERS, TOYS AND BOXES PILED UP AGAINST THE WINDOWS.

contemporary, dramatic yet practical design. When you turn your back on the original design, such as fitting small, fake leaded cottage-type casement windows in a 1970s flat, or running a kitchen worktop past the low windowsill of a Georgian sash window, you are not working with the fabric of the building and are ignoring the heritage of your home. This will lead to clashes in style and design that will never be quite right no matter what interior design scheme you employ.

I have written this book because our homes do not reflect the incalculable shift in the way we live. Housing and home design used to be the ultimate for any architect, but now often only the design of a one-off, multimillion-pound house is seen as award-worthy and prestigious. For me, creating a working, living home where a family can connect, children can be watched at play from the kitchen, a couple or individual can feel rested and inspired, is my ultimate goal.

How to read + draw a plan

The basics of how to look at and understand drawings is key to the confidence you need to achieve what you want from your design and get your voice heard. It is daunting enough to be thrust into a situation where you have a lack of experience or knowledge, but when the situation involves your own money and home it can be terrifying. For me, architecture is a mindset rather than a mysterious dark art.

The fact that we are collectively so nervous and one-step removed from the design process of our homes is symptomatic of the construction industry holding its cards close to its chest for its own preservation. This book is not designed to replace your architect or designer by any stretch of the imagination, and I am a firm believer that our profession brings a vast amount to the (kitchen) table. However, over the years I have noticed that most people have one thing in common when embarking on their own building project – a fear of not having their voice heard, or even knowing what their voice should be saying.

Although on the surface learning how to draw a toilet and a bookcase may seem irrelevant, I truly believe that it is a crucial starting point. Learning how to read and draw a rough plan will quickly help you identify the problem areas and pinch points in your home. These are the fundamentals, the foundations of the knowledge you need. I will add layers to this new understanding so that, when you are sitting with your architect, you can discuss sightlines and aspect with ease. Then, when you are on-site with your builder and he or she is chatting merrily about rads, subfloors and soil vent pipes you will understand the context and therefore be a key part of the conversation.

I am mindful of not creating a dry instructional chapter on surveying and drawing, but sadly there is very little pizazz I can bring to learning how to read and draw a plan. However, if I was sitting there with you in person explaining this stage, I would have most definitely brought cake, so I suggest that you treat yourself to a lovely snack, healthy or otherwise, as you master this crucial skill set.

DESIGN SYMBOLS

1:100

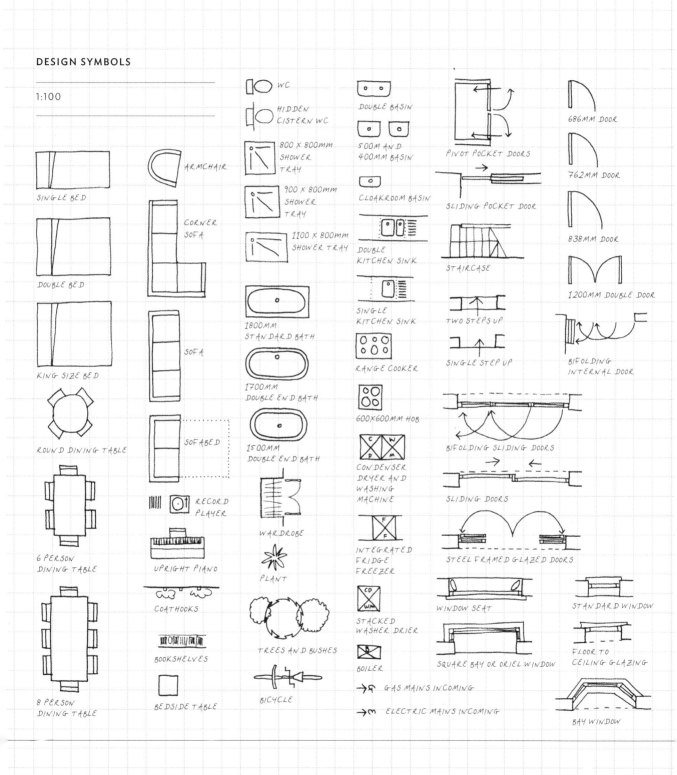

SINGLE BED

DOUBLE BED

KING SIZE BED

ROUND DINING TABLE

6 PERSON DINING TABLE

8 PERSON DINING TABLE

ARMCHAIR

CORNER SOFA

SOFA

SOFABED

RECORD PLAYER

UPRIGHT PIANO

COATHOOKS

BOOKSHELVES

BEDSIDE TABLE

WC

HIDDEN CISTERN WC

800 x 800mm SHOWER TRAY

900 x 800mm SHOWER TRAY

1100 x 800mm SHOWER TRAY

1800MM STANDARD BATH

1700MM DOUBLE END BATH

1500MM DOUBLE END BATH

WARDROBE

PLANT

TREES AND BUSHES

BICYCLE

DOUBLE BASIN

500MM AND 400MM BASIN

CLOAKROOM BASIN

DOUBLE KITCHEN SINK

SINGLE KITCHEN SINK

RANGE COOKER

600x600MM HOB

CONDENSER DRYER AND WASHING MACHINE

INTEGRATED FRIDGE FREEZER

STACKED WASHER DRIER

BOILER

→♭ GAS MAINS INCOMING

→m ELECTRIC MAINS INCOMING

PIVOT POCKET DOORS

SLIDING POCKET DOOR

STAIRCASE

TWO STEPS UP

SINGLE STEP UP

BIFOLDING SLIDING DOORS

SLIDING DOORS

STEEL FRAMED GLAZED DOORS

WINDOW SEAT

SQUARE BAY OR ORIEL WINDOW

686MM DOOR

762MM DOOR

838MM DOOR

1200MM DOUBLE DOOR

BIFOLDING INTERNAL DOOR

STANDARD WINDOW

FLOOR TO CEILING GLAZING

BAY WINDOW

Looking at your plan

Even if you have lived in your home for years, imagine that you are looking at a plan of it for the first time. I find homeowners are often stuck in a rut, fixated on details such as knocking through a particular wall or two. Although these theoretical alterations may seem to be an obvious solution, and may indeed become part of the final layout, by ignoring them you can focus on the design process and open yourself up to new ways of thinking and a fresh set of fully considered ideas. This new perspective will kick-start your creativity, allowing you to think in an architectural way yet retaining the roots of your own needs, desires and practicalities.

The first thing I do when I am given the plan for a house or flat is to rotate it so that I am looking at it as if I am walking in through the front door. This helps me to visualize the flow of the space. Looking at a plan can be quite overwhelming, but by starting at the front door you can step into the layout in your mind.

There is no definitive, universally agreed way to illustrate a floor plan, but there are several drawing conventions that we can play around with to create your own simple, legible drawing.

1. PLAN POSITION

Layout plans are always drawn from above. Imagine you are floating 1 m (3 ft) above the floor and drawing everything you see below you from that position.

2. LOOKING UP

If you turn around and face upward, the beams that are hanging down, lowered ceiling sections and openings are depicted in short, dashed lines. If there is a dimension written on or close to the dashed lines, that will tell you the height of the underside of this element. For example, if there is a beam running across the room that is particularly low, then this will be indicated. Restricted head heights will be shown in rooms with eaves such as attic or loft rooms.

3. DOORS AND WINDOWS

Doors are always drawn open, and I like to draw them with a lovely round arc showing the swing of the door so you can visualize how much space they will take up when opening and closing.

4. INTERNAL AND EXTERNAL WALLS

Thick or solid filled lines show that you are cutting through a wall or structure, whereas thinner lines represent objects below your 1 m- (3 ft-) high vision, such as tables and windowsills.

5. NORTH POINT

Although not always included on layout plans, this aspect is one of the most important elements to help you to understand your existing layout, and will give vital clues to the opportunities and limitations of your design ideas. It is the most important factor in how your design will come together, so if the path of the sun isn't mentioned by the architect or designer you are working with, then perhaps you should ask them why not.

6. STAIRS

Stairs are a bone of contention. I always draw them with the arrow of travel heading up to the highest step. Other plans draw an arrow pointing in either direction and then state 'up' or 'down' to show direction. But I find this confusing, so keep it simple and always remember to point your arrow to the top.

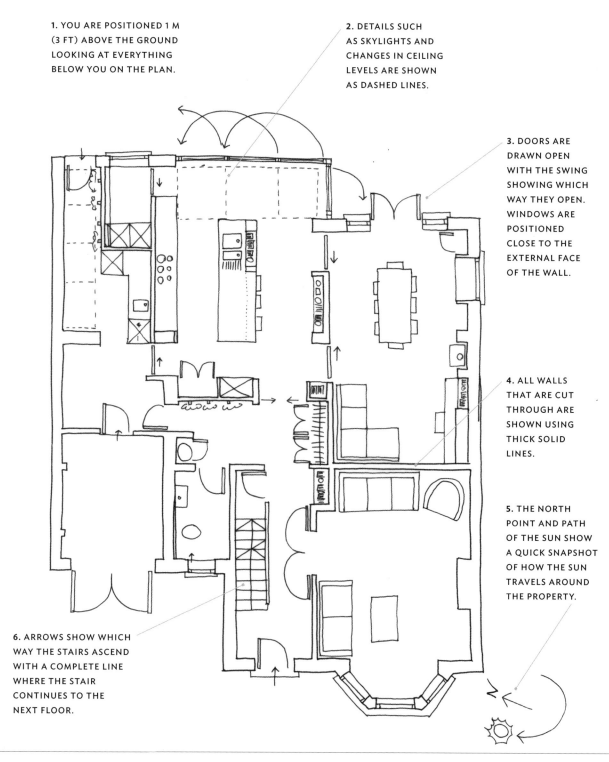

1. YOU ARE POSITIONED 1 M (3 FT) ABOVE THE GROUND LOOKING AT EVERYTHING BELOW YOU ON THE PLAN.

2. DETAILS SUCH AS SKYLIGHTS AND CHANGES IN CEILING LEVELS ARE SHOWN AS DASHED LINES.

3. DOORS ARE DRAWN OPEN WITH THE SWING SHOWING WHICH WAY THEY OPEN. WINDOWS ARE POSITIONED CLOSE TO THE EXTERNAL FACE OF THE WALL.

4. ALL WALLS THAT ARE CUT THROUGH ARE SHOWN USING THICK SOLID LINES.

5. THE NORTH POINT AND PATH OF THE SUN SHOW A QUICK SNAPSHOT OF HOW THE SUN TRAVELS AROUND THE PROPERTY.

6. ARROWS SHOW WHICH WAY THE STAIRS ASCEND WITH A COMPLETE LINE WHERE THE STAIR CONTINUES TO THE NEXT FLOOR.

DP – DOWN PIPE

This is the thinner of the pipes running down the outside of a building and is usually 75 mm (3 in.) wide. Traditionally, it takes rainwater from the gutters to the main underground sewer. These days, if you are adding an extension, the new surface must be drained to a separate soak-away (or attenuation tank to give it its fancy name). This is essentially a hole filled with rubble or a proprietary plastic crate system – the size depends on the surface area of your extension roof – and it allows water to percolate out into the surrounding ground so that no more water enters the sewage system.

RWP – RAIN WATER PIPE

Another term for down pipe. I prefer this term personally. Who doesn't have a favoured term for pipes?

SVP – SOIL VENT PIPE

These are the thicker pipes, typically 110 mm (4.3 in.) wide, taking waste (called soil) from toilets to the sewer. You will often see the toilet connected to the SVP if the pipe is on the outside of the building. The pipe then extends past the last soil connection to ventilate the run down to the underground drains. The top of your SVP must be 900 mm (35.4 in.) away from an opening window to avoid the foul smell of the sewer gently wafting back into your home.

STUB – STUB STACK SYSTEM

We haven't quite left drainage yet. A stub stack is a short soil vent pipe that can't be ventilated to the outside air. As the name suggests, these stubby, cut-off pipes have a one-way ventilation valve on top that looks like a little flat hat. It allows air to be sucked in to ventilate the system, but does not allow any noxious sewer fumes to escape back into the bathroom. That is, when it works. You often find them in much larger buildings, where there isn't an easy route for the SVP to be vented to the outside air.

SFL – STRUCTURAL FLOOR LEVEL

I know it might remind you of the Scottish Football League, but the SFL on drawings denotes the level of the rough structure of your floor, such as the top of the timber joists, concrete slab or suspended block floor. If you are undergoing substantial works, the floors will often be taken away before being replaced and you will need to know the level at which they will go back. When installing the foundations and steel elements of the structure where you have no floor to measure from,

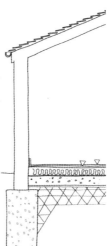

the SFL line is used so you know at what height everything goes. On top of the structural floor level comes the sub-floor level. You never really see sub-floor level on drawings, probably because it also begins with 'S' and no one has come up with an alternative name for it yet so it would just confuse everyone. However, the sub-floor is a sheet material such as plywood or chipboard needed over the rough concrete or block structural floor finish.

FFL – FINISHED FLOOR LEVEL

The FFL indicates the level of the top of your final floor covering such as tiles, wood or carpet. If your existing floor has been removed you may find this scrawled on the wall with a line indicating the level of your finished floor. Being able to see the FFL is critical during 'first fix' when plumbers, electricians and builders install pipes and cables in your walls ready to be connected. They need to know at what height to install them to ensure all the pipes, sockets, windows and kitchen worktops are installed at the right height once your floor is put back. After first fix comes 'second fix'. Once the pipes and cables are connected, the flooring and finishes are in. Second fix involves putting the sanitaryware into the bathrooms, the faceplates on the socket boxes and the units into the kitchen. Second fix is one of the greatest milestones on a building site.

RSJ - ROLLED STEEL JOIST

A structural support beam with an I or H cross section. They are often painted red on-site, this is oxide paint to prevent rusting.

UB - UNIVERSAL BEAM

This is essentially another term for an RSJ. They are interchangeable and your builder, engineer and architect will usually have a preference. But they won't necessarily be the same as each other.

FOUNDS - FOUNDATIONS

Usually shown as a dotted line, the foundation line is often indicated on ground floor drawings to show where they are relative to the walls of your build.

RAD - RADIATOR

Nice and simple.

OSB - ORIENTED STRAND BOARD

Also known as Stirling Board, an OSB is made up of strips of wood, glued and compressed into rigid sheets. It is often used instead of plywood on timber frame structures, extensions and loft dormers. You may recognize the aesthetic of exposed sheets of OSB in trendy coffee shops and bars. I must admit, I am a bit of a fan.

NOGGINS

Noggins are the little horizontal timber struts (above) that connect and stiffen joists and wall studs. In Scotland, noggins are called dwangs.

MH - MANHOLE

I seem to spend half my life looking for manholes around houses to try to work out how the drainage flows in a home. This is something they did not tell me about in architecture school. Drainage is one of the most important fixed points to consider when designing, especially in a house or flat where it is difficult or impossible to move and alter. Manholes are metal plates from 600 x 600 mm (23.6 x 23.6 in.) up to 1200 x 1200 mm (47.2 x 47.2 in.) that cover underground sewer or foul connections. They are usually dotted around the perimeter or side of a house, the first manhole being close to a soil vent stack, and continue out to join the main, communal sewer. Sometimes you can just see the metal frame, instead of a full metal cover so they can be camouflaged in paving or flooring. Having a manhole, even a sealed one, inside the home is no longer allowed.

IL - INVERT LEVEL

The invert level is the depth of the sewer channel. If the invert level is 1 m (3 ft), then that is how far underground it is. The deeper the manhole, the easier it is to get the correct fall on any new drainage pipes connecting into the system in your proposed design.

FALL

Often shown as a gradient or ratio, the fall indicates how steep an element such as a ramp, patio or pipe is laid at. Fall is the distance dropping vertically over the length of distance it takes to drop. A 1 in 40 pipe fall means that for every 40 units of length, the pipe will drop by 1 unit.

IC - INSPECTION CHAMBER

Essentially a mini manhole, with enough space to check on a connection. These are often installed where an existing manhole is covered over in an extension and a new inspection chamber is installed close by to allow continued access.

RP - RODDING POINT

This is a delightfully named drain access point, where you can stick rods down to clear away any blockages in the drainage system. It is usually the diameter of a soil vent pipe and often has a small twist-off cap, branching off the main soil pipe itself.

Drawing your own plan

I always like to start a new layout design by drawing up the existing one. Although they are often rather rough and inaccurate, estate agents' plans do give an indication of how the rooms in your home come together. If you don't have any type of plan, or the inclination or budget for a full-blown measured survey, then drawing your own is a great place to start. One advantage to drawing your own, even if you do it before a full independent survey, is that there is something relatable about a hand-drawn plan. If I am given a professional layout drawing, I always trace over it in my own hand. It is a great way to understand the rooms, and get all those non-standardized details drawn the way you would like them to be, especially the stairs.

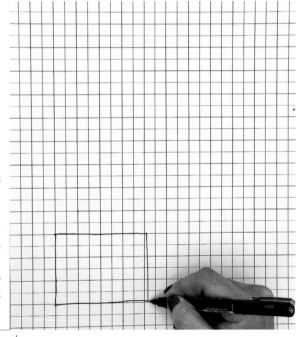

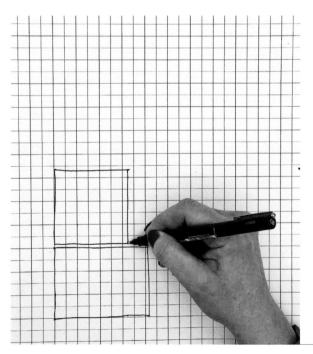

DRAWING YOUR
EXISTING LAYOUT

Starting a survey of your existing home can seem like a formidable task, so I will break it down to make it as easy and simple as possible.

Take a blank sheet of paper – plain or with a grid to help guide you – then start with the basic shape of a room which, more often than not, is fairly rectangular. Even where the basic shape of a room is interrupted by a fireplace or a corner has been taken out, visualize the outline of the room and draw that. If it is an odd shape, for example a wedge, then estimate the smaller and longer lengths to give you an accurate outline.

Now move next door and draw the next room. Choose a room that shares a wall with your first room, such as the back or side wall. Again, if none of your walls align then don't worry, just estimate how far it is set back or forward and we will tackle the exact positioning in the next stage. Once you have completed all your rooms, you will have a series of outline boxes indicating the basic existing layout. Do not worry about doors or windows at this point, the aim is to get the overall layout down. I like to draw a second line to show the dividing wall, so each room has its own box. In this way you are already bringing some wall thickness into your plan. You can measure the thickness of the wall later, but for now give an indication of whether it is just a standard internal wall or maybe a nice big thick one.

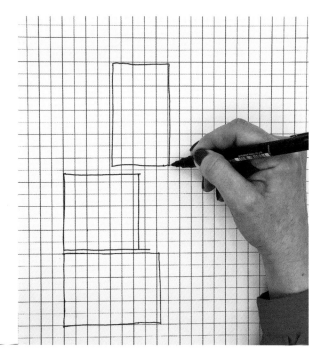

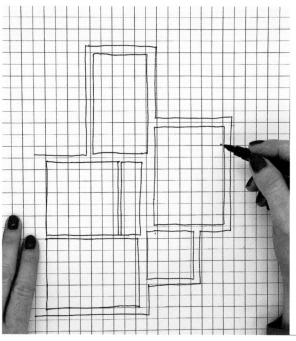

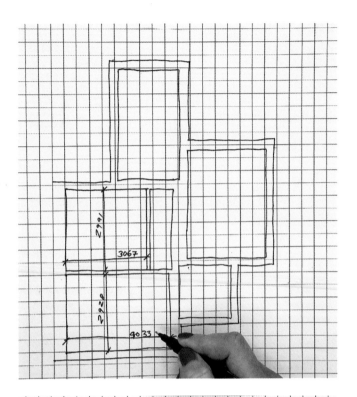

DIMENSIONS, DIMENSIONS, DIMENSIONS

Now we need to measure the rooms. Conventionally in the UK, millimetres are the unit of choice on architectural drawings. Using the boxy layout plan, I like to return to the first room and use a laser tape measure to take two full measurements across the length and the width of the room. For more unconventionally shaped rooms, such as those with deep bay windows or with a chunk taken out of a corner, you will need to make a note of each length on your drawing. Where a room wall does not line up with the adjacent room, the best way to measure its position is to take a fixed point in both rooms, for example the inside of a door frame. You can then transpose the distance from this fixed point to the walls in both rooms to your final survey drawing. You can leave all the door and window measurements for now, and avoid over filling your layout with dimensions. But if this isn't your first rodeo, add the positioning dimensions for the wall openings now.

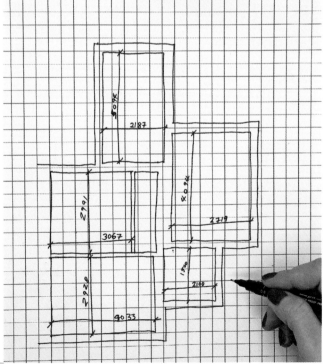

A QUESTION OF SCALE

Once you have annotated your initial layout drawing with measurements, it is time to use the survey as a basis to draw an accurate design onto graph or grid paper. On graph paper, work out what you are going to set as your 1 m or 1000 mm (39.3 in.) scale size; it is usually 10 mm (0.4 in.) to signify 1 m (39.3 in.). This will give you an overall scale of 1:50, meaning that any line you draw will equate to 50 times that size in reality. Most three- or four-bedroom houses and flats will fit comfortably onto an A3 page at this 1:50 scale.

So, starting at your favourite corner, draw your rooms to size connecting them with the wall width in-between. Again, don't worry about windows and doors at this stage, we will get to those. Although it seems fairly labour intensive, it is quite fun to see how the spaces come together and it's a great way to get a real understanding of how your home works. The more you draw, the easier it becomes, and this insight into your existing home is a crucial step in your design journey.

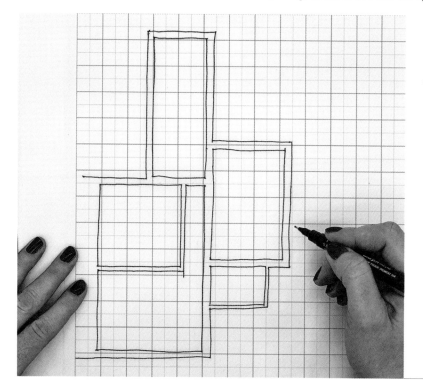

Windows, doors and details – bringing your plan to life

It is the features and details that bring a plan drawing to life and help you to see the context of each room. Positioning the windows and doors is particularly helpful when gaining a good understanding of the existing layout, and this will help you to get your head around the plan when you start sketching out your proposed ideas.

Again, there is no standard way to illustrate these elements, but remember, you are cutting through your plan at roughly 1 m (3 ft) high, so windows can be sketched simply with little rectangle blocks connected by three lines. Each block signifies the two sides of the window frame at each end of the window opening, and these in turn are drawn together with three lines; the outside two representing the window frame that you are looking down on and the middle line the glass that you are cutting through. You can also show any turns, bends or curves in your window, as well as any big posts or corner elements by adding another rectangular block highlighting the frame position. The doors are a little bit more straightforward. You generally draw the door leaf, the actual opening bit, sitting open; and I like to draw on a lovely curve showing the way the door swings. Use small arrows to indicate where and how sliding, pocket, bifold or unconventional doors open.

Once your doors and windows are in position, you may see many extraneous lines left over from setting out your layout. Trace over your work onto a sheet of plain tracing paper to create a clear drawing of the main walls, doors and windows, and you will be surprised at how quickly your initial sketches will become your own elegant architectural drawing.

There will always be crucial items of furniture, tables and chairs, sideboards and heirlooms, sofas and armchairs, both universal or unique to you, that require space in your home. You can trace and develop my drawings of typical pieces and add to your plan as you go. You can cut them out and move them around your existing layout as your ideas move forward. I really like the fact that it feels like putting furniture into a dolls house. I hope you enjoy it too.

A CLEAR EXISTING PLAN IS A KEY STARTING POINT FOR ANY DESIGN. DRAWING IN YOUR FURNITURE, KITCHEN LAYOUT AND EVEN PLANTS, HELPS BRING YOUR LAYOUT TO LIFE AND ADDS A SENSE OF SCALE TO YOUR HOME.

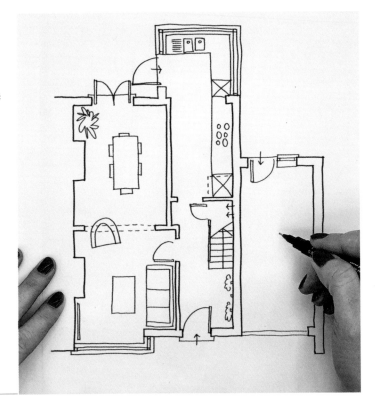

Walking through your plan

Let's start at the front door of your house or flat. No matter the idiosyncrasies of your individual plan, rotate it so that the entrance door is toward the bottom of the page or screen so that you have your back to the front door. Now, trace your finger up the page to indicate how you commence your walk through the space. You can then see if you have a blank wall or door in front of you, or any views through or down corridors. You can also ascertain what is behind various walls, what you could be looking at, and the potential for viewpoints as you 'walk' around the plan.

You will start to understand that what is in front of you on the plan reflects the four walls of your space. At the front door, you can start to see whether you are looking at a view of the kitchen sink or perhaps, if you are lucky, a tantalizing glimpse of a toilet.

Take a marker pen and draw on your usual routes of circulation. Draw the way from the front door through to the kitchen, the kitchen through to the dining space, and the living room to the bottom of the stairs if you have them. This gives an insight into how you use your home and where it is not working. I will go into this in greater detail in the second part of this book, showing you how to analyze these lines and squiggles to identify dead areas within your existing layout and how to maximize your space when you embark on your proposed design.

SECTIONS + ELEVATIONS

Sections are drawings that cut through the building, like a slice cut from a cake to show the layers. The slice where the section is drawn is shown on the plan with little arrows usually labelled with letters. Elevations are the sides of the outside of the building drawn flat-on with no perspective.

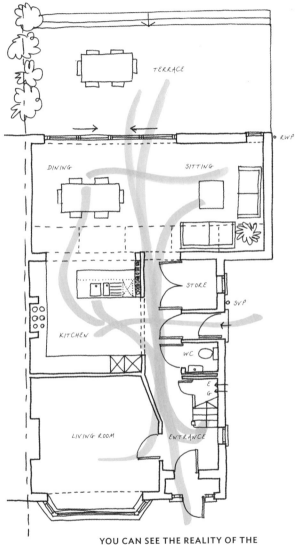

YOU CAN SEE THE REALITY OF THE VIEW THROUGH THE PLAN. STANDING IN THE ENTRANCE, YOU CAN SEE SNEAK PEAKS OF THE KITCHEN ISLAND, DINING AND THROUGH TO THE GARDEN. THE SINK IS SHIELDED FROM YOUR INITIAL VIEW, AND THE WALL BOTH CONTAINS THE KITCHEN AND GIVES A FEELING OF FLOW THROUGH TO THE HEART OF THE HOME.

Establishing a brief

I am often given design briefs that are pages long, listing everything about the homeowners' lives, from their children's hobbies to the name of their dog. While this is all very valuable information, for me establishing a brief is more about creating a feeling.

Drawing up a balanced wish list of your ultimate desires and practical needs will help you to communicate how you want to feel when you walk through the front door, or how your home will adapt from a busy working week to relaxed weekend gatherings.

Your project brief can be solely for you, or a key document to be shared with your architect or designer. By revisiting, editing and collating it in the early stages, just like you would a mood board, you will create a final brief that succinctly outlines the bones of your dream home.

When you sit down to start writing your brief, take a step back and look at your home as if you have never seen it before. Forget all your preconceptions and existing niggles and start afresh. The best thing about this approach is that it enables you to establish a brief that is scalable. Whether you are looking to remodel your entire home, or just a single room, this method will give you a comprehensive framework to initiate the exciting process of the design itself.

Establishing the brief is about working out what you can and cannot do, and also setting the parameters of what you want and do not want from your home. When your brief is clarified, you can set about putting in your initial sketch design ideas. After reading this chapter, you will have an outline of your daily routine relative to your home and its rooms, where the problem areas are and what you need to change. You will be able to recognize the areas of warmth and comfort, the spaces you gravitate to during the day and how all of this changes throughout the week.

THIS BRIGHT LIVING ROOM WITH TALL, SOUTH-FACING SASH WINDOWS IS FILLED WITH DIRECT SUNSHINE DURING THE LATE MORNING AND EARLY AFTERNOON IN BOTH SUMMER AND WINTER. BECAUSE THE ROOM IS SINGLE-ASPECT, THAT IS WITH WINDOWS ONLY FACING ONE DIRECTION, IT DOES NOT ENJOY THE BENEFIT OF THE EVENING GLOW AS THE SUN SETS IN THE WEST.

The outline brief

There is no hard-and-fast rule to writing a brief. It should create a narrative around your desires, as well as state your needs and the parameters of your existing home rather than be a tick-box exercise. However, I have broken down the conversation I always have with homeowners at the beginning of every new project I undertake to give an outline of how to structure your own brief.

1. WANTS + NEEDS
Your dreams and design aspirations, lifestyle and daily routine that must be considered and catered for within your home.

2. SITE + ASPECT
How and where natural light and sunshine impacts your home and its surroundings.

3. OCCUPANCY
How your layout must change and adapt to cater for expanding and contracting numbers of people within the home.

4. BUDGET
What you want to spend and how and where to best spend it.

5. FIXED POINT + SERVICES
From structure to drainage, planning restrictions to gas meters, these are elements that can restrict and become the design parameters to work within.

1. What do you want?

So simple, yet so complex. Focus on how you want your home to work for you and establish the practicalities of your daily life. Picture what you require to make your life flow with ease, whether that is great storage or a clear kitchen island. It is often the simple things that bring a space alive.

The term 'the heart of the home' is ambiguous and even overused. For me, it is the area or place that you love and spend most of your time in. This should reflect the family as a whole and as individuals, and is an element that makes a space special for you. It can be as simple as a view, a kitchen table, sunlight or a feeling of cosiness. Creating a special space is not about labelling, it is about understanding what makes an area feel right. You cannot just write 'this is the heart of the home' and expect it to become that. If you do not gravitate toward this area now, trying to plan it as the heart of the home will be tricky.

The more time we spend at home, the more we realize where it is not working for us. It may be a lack of storage; you may be frustrated that you cannot see out to your garden when you are in the kitchen, and as a result the feeling of separation within your own four walls becomes apparent. Write all the failings of your home down to incorporate them into your list of wants and needs.

Your brief is not just about reflecting daily life in your home, it is also about the look and feel you want to achieve, including the materials and finishes. Considering these at this stage might seem to be jumping the gun but I am sure, if you are anything like me, you will have an idea about the style of home that you want before you even put pen to paper.

Usually a builder's initial, ballpark quote includes standard costs for every element, from sockets to glazing. It is therefore worth flagging any potentially expensive or unusual items early on, so they can be accommodated within the budget. For example, you may have set your heart on real marble worktops or would like to install an air source heat pump. You can look for savings elsewhere to allow your budget to stretch to your design aspiration.

The materials you choose can affect the rooms and spaces within your home. Certain fixtures and fittings will have an impact on the fabric of your build, and it is important to bear them in mind at this point.

YOUR BRIEF SHOULD INCLUDE ANY ITEMS THAT YOU LOVE AND WANT TO KEEP, SUCH AS A BEAUTIFUL STAIRCASE OR FIREPLACE. INCORPORATING EXISTING ORIGINAL FEATURES SUCH AS CEILING ROSES AND CORNICES INTO YOUR DESIGN CAN IMPACT ON HOW AND WHERE YOU CAN OPEN UP OR REMOVE INTERNAL WALLS, SO THEY SHOULD BE CONSIDERED FROM THE START.

CEILINGS AND ROOF

Whether the ceiling is the focal point of your design through clever use of light, height, geometry and style, or you would prefer it to blend seamlessly into your interior design scheme by extending your paint and wallpaper upward, considering how you want to integrate it is key to creating a holistic and complete design.

Always think in straight lines. You can bring a feeling of bespoke detailing, even with the most cost-effective construction, if the lines of your ceiling and any roof glazing align with the features below it. However, you do not need to be slavish to this. I love asymmetry, and finding one clear line that runs from floor to ceiling can harmonize the finish. Changes in ceiling height will define the zones and spaces below them, especially when coupled with glazing that allows in natural light from above.

Kitchens work well with high ceiling levels. The sound quality in a high, raked ceiling can be lively and bright, and this will reflect and enhance the kitchen as the bustling heart of the home. The extra height can give a cooling effect and enable ventilation. In living rooms, the echoey sound of a double height ceiling can be tempered by soft furnishings while retaining a sense of grandeur.

Treating the ceiling as the 'fifth wall' will help you to envisage the space as a whole, either as part of the interior decoration scheme or a more architecturally expressive design. Incorporating the ceiling into your design from the outset can elevate the final finish within the home. In a warm roof build up, where the insulation is contained above the joists, it allows the joists to be exposed to allow the geometry of the carpentry to become an integral part of the design. Joists can be kept uniform and linear or, working with your engineer, the layout can be more sculptural to bring a unique element to your plans.

Lighting too will enhance any exposed structure, bringing yet another dimension to your ceiling.

WALLS

The points where walls join and abut often feature steps and misalignments. These are great opportunities to introduce storage or shelving nooks to create a flush line. Built-in shelves in showers and bathrooms are simple but often forgotten details that minimize the need for extraneous shelving.

Windows are fairly straightforward to thermally upgrade, whereas walls are not. Damp, cold, mouldy walls are a pervasive problem, whether they are in Georgian piles or 1980s bungalows. We tend to focus on technological options to make our homes greener, such as photovoltaics, ground and air source heat pumps, triple glazing and Passivhaus. But we pay less attention to the effect of the breathability of our homes. Lime is one of the oldest building materials in the world. Unlike cement and gypsum plaster, lime plaster is breathable and naturally absorbs ambient moisture, helping to solve damp and mould problems. Lime render and lime mortar are softer than cement and therefore allow natural movement and do not damage the fabric of the building. Due to the hardness and rigidity of cement – the very characteristics that made it so popular – any water that gets in when it cracks and degrades has no escape and starts to soak the stone or brick wall underneath it, separating any render and allowing rot to set in.

Today, the manufacture of cement accounts for 8 per cent of global CO_2 emissions. When compared to the aviation industry, which makes up 2 per cent of CO_2 emissions, you can see the huge ongoing environmental cost. In contrast, lime production is considered carbon neutral as the CO_2 emitted during its manufacture is reabsorbed by lime mortar and render over the years as it chemically converts back into limestone, getting stronger as a result. With the addition of small amounts of cement and perlite, lime mortar, render and lime-based alternatives to concrete, such as hempcrete, are becoming cheaper, set more quickly, are more robust, self-finishing and, crucially, naturally insulating. Yet these innovations are regularly dismissed as an expensive unknown quantity.

WINDOWS AND DOORS

The style of your windows and doors will have a huge impact on the overall look of your home, inside and out. Timber looks beautiful, yet has the burden of maintenance. Aluminium will be hassle-free in the long term, yet the power-coated frames can look rather flat. Doors and windows made from uPVC have come a long way, and heritage-style sliding sash windows have been advocated by the Royal Institute of British Architects.

Composite windows – aluminium on the outside and timber on the inside – are a great compromise to create sleek, contemporary lines on your elevations with the warmth of painted timber indoors. Steel-framed glazing is elegant and looks good everywhere.

Handles and other ironmongery are the most important part of any door as you use them often. Even if you go for a more cost-effective plain door leaf, always choose a fire door. Standard fire doors are labelled FD30 or FD60, indicating that they withstand fire for 30 and 60 minutes respectively. They are, by their very nature, much more solid, heavier doors, and even if you do not need fire doors in certain areas to comply with building control, they feel more substantial to use and only cost a fraction more than hollow or foam-filled doors.

FLOORING

Your choice of flooring will depend on the feel and finish you want to achieve and the height you have to play with. A limited build up means that you must try to minimize the finished floor thickness in order not to impact on your finished ceiling height. Underfloor heating is a great, lower-energy option. Infrared heating is a great solution too, where underfloor heating or retrofitting a heating system is not an option. Infrared heats objects rather than the air and therefore it is great in already damp areas, basements and utility rooms as it does not increase humidity.

If you are going for a timber or natural finish such as cork, then ensure you get plenty of samples and walk on them with your shoes on to check the longevity of the finished surface.

It is possible to install great-looking engineered timber boards that have a very thin veneer of real wood. But bear in mind that if the wooden surface is damaged the wood layer will not be thick enough to sand down to make it look great again.

If you are going to tile a floor – I have a soft spot for wood-effect tiles – then always use an epoxy grout. It is more expensive than standard grout but, unlike natural grouts, can be cleaned quickly and easily making maintenance less time-consuming. Setting out is really important in your floors. Similar to the straight lines that I talk about in skylights, walls and windows, think about the lines on your floors and walls and the position of any cut lines in tiles or floorboards to give a clean finish that looks good throughout your home.

CREATING A LONG SLOT OF GLAZING IN A CEILING IS A GREAT WAY TO FLOOD A SPACE WITH NATURAL LIGHT AND A DRAMATIC WAY TO JOIN OLD TO NEW. BECAUSE THE SLIM, HORIZONTAL GLAZING IS AT A HIGH LEVEL IT WILL MINIMIZE ANY EFFECT OF OVERHEATING, EVEN IN A ROOM THAT FACES DUE SOUTH.

2. Sunshine, light + aspect

In architecture and design, the term aspect is commonly used to describe the direction that your home faces and how sunlight falls onto your property.

In the next section, we will look at designing around your home's aspect. I will show you how to look at the path of the sun, where it can be brought into a proposed layout and how it changes during the day and seasons.

Whether you have lived in your home for 45 years, or you are trying to establish whether a flat that has just come onto the market has the potential to become your dream home, find a satellite image of the property and any surrounding gardens. In this bird's-eye view, rotate your floor plan in the same direction as your home to allow you to establish the north point on your layout. Use it to draw an arrowed arc from east to west to give you a simple representation of the path of the sun through the day.

Where it rises, sets and, importantly, where it comes into your home or, as the case may be, where it does not.

Sunrise and sunset times and the specific path of the sun vary greatly across the seasons and your geographical position on the globe. However, this quick method gives a great snapshot to guide you deeper into the brief. You can see where sunlight falls into your home or garden, and identify any potential hot spots that you gravitate toward alongside views out.

3. Friends, family + occupancy

Occupancy is not just a quick body count. Whether you are on your own, starting a family or at a point in life where you are looking to downsize, your core family unit is crucial, not only in terms of numbers but if there are any specialist needs, mobility requirements or future-proofing to bear in mind. If you want this home to be your place for years to come, what vague plans do you have for the future and how could they impact on your needs? In addition, think about how your home expands. Do you entertain a lot and host gatherings? How do you picture those sunny party afternoons and cosy autumnal dinner parties, or is

your focus more on creating a cocoon-like escape from the world?

Think about your daily routines. Do you just grab a coffee and go, or is there a working from home element to your week? Are you desperate to have evening meals around the dinner table or out in the garden, only to find that more often than not you end up sitting in front of the television? It is startling to see how badly laid-out homes are so often working against their occupants, not allowing them to live the way they desire. This exercise will allow you to move away from the existing problems and focus on the end point of design; how you *want* to live. The jigsaw puzzle of architecture is getting from where you are, to where you want to be. On budget.

STORAGE DOESN'T NEED TO BE HIDDEN AWAY BEHIND CUPBOARD DOORS. IF YOU ENTERTAIN A LOT, HAVING BEAUTIFUL YET QUICKLY ACCESSIBLE STORAGE IS KEY TO RETAINING A CLUTTER-FREE ENTRANCE, NO MATTER HOW MANY GUESTS YOU ARE ENTERTAINING.

4. Budget + costs

'So, what is your budget?' This question is always a bit of a conversation stopper, so I like to bring it in once we have established the dream vision. Whether you have a fixed amount of money or are calculating your budget based on the equity of your home, ensure it is a realistic figure and know what you want to achieve with it. You may only need a basic plaster finish that you can take forward once the builders leave, or you may want a full turnkey finish, leaving you nothing to do other than to enjoy your home.

Pricing in the construction industry can be volatile and varies up and down the UK, within Europe and the world. For a rough outline budget for a standard plaster finish, the general rule of thumb is £1,400 to £1,700 ($1,600 to $2,000) per m² for new-build works and £1,100 to £1,300 ($1,200 to $1,500) per m² for interior works. As you can imagine, any specialist finishes or expensive detailing may come in addition to this but, likewise, economic use of materials can also bring down the overall project cost. Once you have a figure in mind, whether it is completely fixed or fairly flexible, write it down, highlighting areas where you would like to spend a bit more, such as a fabulous kitchen, and areas you are happy to save on.

Establishing the position of fixed elements such as drainage, which you will need to work with, is key to ensuring your budget remains on track with as few expensive surprises as possible.

Working with your designer, architect and/or builder will help you maximize your budget and create a bespoke space for less. They may have preferred, cost-effective suppliers for basic items such as sanitaryware or door blanks that you can take advantage of, leaving you free to shop around for your own choice of brassware and door handles. The elements in the home that you touch regularly are the most important ones to get right. They don't need to break the bank, but money spent on quality items here is always a good investment. Reclaimed and vintage ironmongery can work exceptionally well with plain, off-the-shelf doors.

Once you have an initial price from your builder, take a detailed look through it and do not assume everything is automatically included. The contractor should be transparent about their costings, what they have included and what they expect you to cover, and this should be crystal clear from the start.

I have seen instances where builders have been vague with their pricing, and surreptitiously omit the cost of the skirting boards and door architraves, making the quote seem competitive when it is not. Comments such as 'client to supply' or 'fix only' next to a cost means that there are a few holes in the budget that will need to be covered by you, so it is imperative you know this before any contract is agreed, and be sure to add any additional costs to your overall budget. It can be a bit of a balancing act to get a fair quotation. The builder will add an additional mark-up fee to some of the materials they supply to cover the time spent organizing, buying and supplying those goods. These mark-ups will form part of their overall profit on a job, so ensure that your builder is happy for you to supply your own bathroom suite or kitchen, for example, as your taking advantage of seasonal sales may adversely impact their profit. It is important to ensure these details are ironed out as part of the final quotation. You both need to be happy and open with costings, if there is trust between you at the start, it will go a long way to creating a harmonious relationship. That is not always the case, but it is good to start on a positive footing. No pun intended.

My final note is about choosing your builder. Always – always – check their references. Telephone homeowners they have worked with previously to chat about their experiences. As I am sure you know, the building process is very rarely a smooth-running and joyous experience. Getting first-hand insight about how your potential builder deals with the inevitable stresses and strains of running a job, and its impact on the homeowner, is crucial. At the end of the day, your builder is going to be in your home for weeks or months, and it is a strange and intrusive relationship that works best when you get on.

5. Fixed points + services

The fixed points in your home are the elements that cannot be moved or removed easily – or even at all – such as bathroom connections, mains utilities or communal spaces and stairs. While in theory everything can be moved, doing so can be tricky, expensive and increase timings and uncertainty, so working with rather than against them is the strategy I usually adopt. These objects become part of the design process, and establishing where they are and working them into your layout is a great way to keep costs down, especially when you are working with a restricted budget. Other considerations come into play too. Maybe you have just had a new bathroom suite installed, or fancy new integrated wardrobes built. These will become elements to integrate as part of the puzzle.

The soil vent pipe that connects your toilet and bathroom fittings to the sewer, the incoming electricity and gas mains and meters, the boiler and heating system can all be moved and altered if essential, but remember if you are in a shared house or flat, these elements will become absolute fixed points within any new design layouts. Consider them to be a feature of the design, although not in a 'box them in and cover them in fancy wallpaper'

kind of way, it is more about ways to inventively integrate them. For example, if I know that the gas and electricity meters are under the stairs and I want to rejig the access upstairs, then I ensure they are untouched, and I seek to incorporate them into floor to ceiling storage cupboards instead. Boilers and soil vent pipes can be moved, but where possible try to move the proposed boiler position directly above or below the existing one to keep relocation costs to a minimum, introducing a section of wall, post or shelving to hide the immovable object. If your heating system is old and you know it needs to be updated, then it is a great opportunity to rationalize the long runs of pipes and ducting.

By bringing any new boiler or hot water system together, you are also

LOCATE AND MARK UP THE FIXED POINTS ON YOUR PLAN. HERE THEY REMAIN IN THE SAME POSITION ON BOTH THE ORIGINAL LAYOUT AND THE NEW DESIGN.

future-proofing for later works such as adding solar hot water, photovoltaics, air- or ground-source heat pumps.

The need for large steel beams supporting vast structural openings can be minimized by cleverly incorporating supporting walls or posts into doorways, bookshelves or elements such as a kitchen island. Rather than just a post in the middle of your beautiful open-plan space, integrating it into a semi-open shelving system will give the illusion of wide-open spaces and clean-line design, but give additional storage and visual separation as well as a simplified structural scheme.

The construction of your floor is also crucial. If you have solid concrete slab floors, incredible parquet or an original tiled floor finish, or if you are

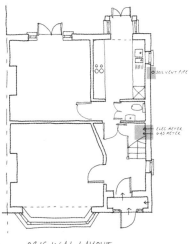

ORIGINAL LAYOUT

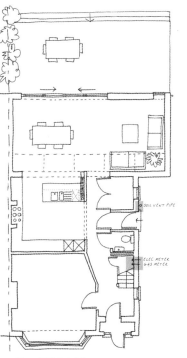

FINISHED LAYOUT

positioned above another apartment for example, then you will be limited as to where you can break through your floor to move your drainage connections. Where there is a cavity underneath your finished floor, moving sinks, basins and toilet connections becomes a lot easier with that freedom of space underneath.

It is important to consider the non-physical fixed points too: rules and regulations. It goes without saying that all proposed building work must comply with both national and regional planning and building regulations, but there are variations across the country and around the world. You may be in a conservation area or very close to one, in a listed building or the green belt. When it comes to building work, there are stringent rules in these areas. If you are in the green belt, there are restrictions on the increased floor area of your proposals that are usually set at 30–35 per cent of the existing floor area as it stood in 1948. This date is important, especially if you are seeking to maximize the footprint of your home. If your house is older than this, a Victorian or Georgian property for example, you must show that any attached garage or extension was built before 1948, even if it was rebuilt at a later date. To do this you should search the historical database of the records held by Ordnance Survey to get a definitive footprint of your home as it stood at this critical date.

Whether you are building a tiny extension or a new-build mansion, read your local council's design guide, so you can quickly

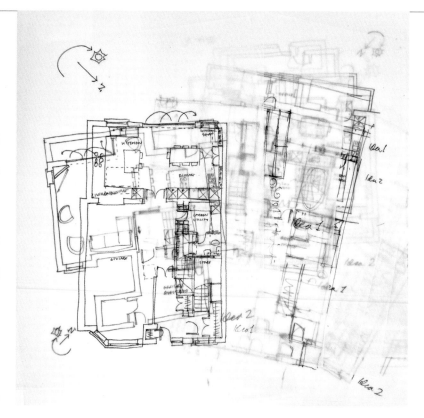

establish what is and what is not acceptable in your area and that may need to be incorporated as part of your brief. I say 'quickly', but it can get rather tedious. However, a couple of precious hours spent absorbing what is architecturally acceptable in your area will allow you to embark on your design with confidence.

All of these fixed points, whether they are physically present or part of the relevant planning restrictions, will form part of the brief, and you will need to integrate them as an element of the design, whether you are working on your own or with an architect or technician.

Brief into drawings

The next stages of design are exciting and exhilarating. I still take hours and hours, make pages and pages of tracing ideas and thoughts, with lines and walls demolished and rebuilt until a design solution starts to emerge. After more than 15 years as a qualified architect, I still get goosebumps when a layout comes together and I see the flow and light that I know will work for the homeowner. So, I hope you have got a lot of ink in your pen, because we are going to start sketching.

GETTING STARTED

With any home design project, whether you have lived in your place for years or you are looking at a property speculatively, this checklist will ensure you have everything you need to get started and see your space objectively using your new design eyes.

YOUR SITE PLAN

The site plan is the layout drawing of your property along with any neighbouring houses, buildings or features. Depending on the size of your home it can be purchased from a mapping site for around £30 ($35). This plan will be used for planning application submissions, so it is worth having a copy from the start of your design project.

BIRDS-EYE VIEW

An up-to-date satellite image showing your house or flat adds context to a site plan. Even if you have lived in your home for years, a detailed bird's-eye view is a brilliant way to see your surroundings in an objective way. It also shows the extent of any neighbouring extensions or developments, enabling you to gauge what is possible in your area.

PATH OF THE SUN

Most Ordnance Survey plans are orientated with north pointing to the top of the map. Drawing on the north point arrow with a curved path of the sun from east to west instantly gives you a snapshot of the path of the sun around your home, highlighting potential sunny spots, gloomy corners or adjacent buildings, structures or trees that may overshadow you.

LASER OR TAPE MEASURE

In order to carry out an initial survey of your home, you will need a tape measure. Laser tapes are ideal as they are quick, accurate to the millimetre and you can pick up a decent one for under £40 ($46). A manual tape measure will work, but can be a pain over larger distances. However they are still indispensable for measuring smaller elements such chimney breasts or short sections of wall under a few centimetres that your laser will not be able to calculate.

DRAWING PENS

I love drawing in ink. I avoid pencils as the lighter lines don't show through tracing paper as clearly as pen does. Have confidence and remember not every single line needs to count. I go through an inordinate amount of tracing paper, drawing and redrawing. Without those mistakes and daft ideas I wouldn't be able to progress and get to the final layout. Both 0.5 mm (0.02 in.) and 0.8 mm (0.03 in.) ink pens are great to sketch with; they don't need to be expensive either.

PAPER AND PADS

Both A3 tracing paper and grid paper are essential (at 420 x 297 mm/16.5 x 11.7 in., A3 is twice the size of A4). The majority of home layouts will fit comfortably onto an A3 page when drawn at 1:50 scale. This means that a 20 mm (0.8 in.) line on your drawing will represent 1 m (39.3 in.) in reality, and is therefore 50 times smaller. For footprints that don't fit comfortably onto a sheet of A3 paper, you can either move up to A2, or stick with A3 and change your scale to 1:100. This will be half the size of 1:50 and so 10 mm (0.4 in.) represents 1 m in reality. You can buy pads of A3 paper printed with a grid of 10 mm (0.4 in.) squares. If you are drawing at 1:50 scale, a 10 mm (0.4 in.) line will equal 500 mm (19.6 in.) in reality. I don't use a ruler to draw straight lines; I put the tracing paper on top of the grid paper and use the lines as a guide. I find it makes the drawing quicker and more fluid.

START YOUR BRIEF

Don't be afraid to get your main objectives down early. Your later, more detailed brief will probably change and morph as the project goes on, so it is good to record your initial desires from the outset. Sometimes even the most basic requirements can get forgotten in the excitement and seemingly endless design decisions. I don't know about you, but when I head to an interiors store without a clear list, I just end up buying up all the faux peonies and huge glass vases.

Cracking common design problems

design *noun* A plan or drawing produced to show the look and function or workings of a building, garment, or other object before it is made.

The word 'design' is so all-encompassing, yet we are often told that simplicity is the key to good design. It seems such a strange dichotomy. It can feel overwhelming to look at the design of anything, especially your home, in its entirety. In this chapter, I will break down the process of design into understandable and manageable sections, from how and where to start, the questions to ask yourself, and how to start unpicking the problem areas so that you can unlock the design solution that is right for you and your home.

All too often we are focused on the wow factor, or creating an *Instagrammable* home, the idea of house envy and house shame. But this is not the true essence of what it is to design a home.

We are so used to idealized, stylized home photos and, I must confess, that I have fallen victim to envy too, and it makes me feel quite uncomfortable. For me, it is akin to the pervasive practice of Photoshopping models' faces and bodies on the pages of fashion magazines and the use of filters on social media. This impossible vision of unobtainable beauty leads us to feel inadequate, paving the way for people to spend their cash on serums and treatments that are advertized alongside the images. When it comes to our homes, scrolling through gorgeous,

spotlessly clean, styled rooms should be a source of joy and inspiration, not shame. It is always good to remember that behind every shot there is a photographer, stylist and a knackered homeowner who spent the last three days before the shoot touching up and polishing every surface and holding back a tide of vases, trinkets and household clutter that did not make that shot.

The reason I love being an architect, and one of the reasons I am writing this book, is to help people crack that illusive design problem: making a home that works for them and their lives. By solving the multitude of ongoing problems with our current homes, we are making peoples' lives easier and more enjoyable. Our homes must work with us, not against us. It is all about enhancing your space, time and, ultimately, life.

Armed with the new knowledge and understanding of the language and symbols of plan drawings, the next steps will begin to fall into place like a perfectly played game of Tetris. Understanding my thought processes will help you see your home not as a daunting project but as a series of puzzles, a jigsaw that can be broken down into logical design ideas and solutions. Solving the problems in your home is one of the most exciting things you can do. It is where you live and spend most of your time, so getting it right is fundamental to life.

THE WALL BETWEEN THIS KITCHEN
AND DINING ROOM WAS OPENED UP
TO GIVE A PRACTICAL, LIGHT-FILLED
ROOM IN A TRADITIONAL GEORGIAN,
CLOSED-PLAN LAYOUT. FOCUS IS
PULLED THROUGH THE DINING
ROOM TO THE VIEW BEYOND.

Untangling the past

The layout of nearly every house or flat can be placed in a clear historical period, but this can get rather fuzzy around the edges. Having spent the last decade dedicated to home design, it has become evident to me that many extended homes follow a clear pattern. These characteristics have appeared and mutated over the centuries due to population increases, the growth of conurbations, technological advances and geopolitical factors such as wars and the impact of the privatization of national house building.

If you have mentally switched off at the sight of the word 'geopolitical', then don't worry, that is the first and last time I will mention it. Well, almost. I think it is important to know the era your home was built, what decisions were made when doing so, and why. Economics is the biggest factor in understanding why we have such a plethora of badly laid out homes. In our towns and cities, large homes that were built as symbols of wealth, have often been carved up to create self-contained apartments. Down the ages, housing has been provided as a response to what was going on in the country and the world. In cities such as Liverpool, Manchester and Birmingham, vast

TYPICAL HOUSE PLANS THROUGH THE AGES

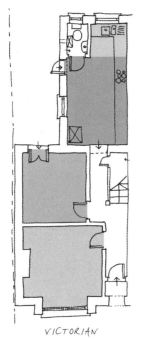

VICTORIAN

ALL THE ROOMS ARE SEPARATED OFF BY CLOSED DOORS THAT OPEN INTO THE SPACE. FEATURE BAY WINDOWS AND FIREPLACES ARE A FOCUS OF WELL-PROPORTIONED ROOMS.

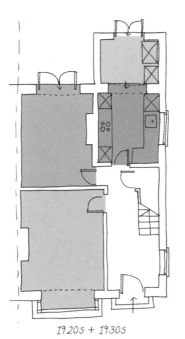

1920S + 1930S

SIMILAR TO THE VICTORIAN PLAN BUT WIDER AND SHORTER, WITH A SMALL GALLEY KITCHEN TO THE REAR WHICH IS NOT CONNECTED TO THE DINING ROOM.

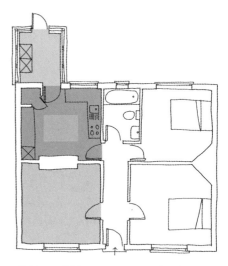

1930S + 1940S BUNGALOW + PREFABS

SINGLE LEVEL WITH A DARK CORRIDOR LINKING ROOMS. BUILT BETWEEN THE WARS, FEATURES SUCH AS BAY WINDOWS WERE NOT INCLUDED, YET FIREPLACES STILL HEATED EACH ROOM.

swathes of two-up-two-down, back-to-back terraced housing was quickly built during industrialization to accommodate the influx of workers. With land at a premium, facilities for bathing and laundry were often shared between an entire street.

Fast-forward several generations, to the 1960s and 1970s, when homeowners demanded space for recent inventions such as the fridge, freezer and washing machine in their homes. Finding somewhere to house them became a huge issue. It had just been possible to squeeze in a family bathroom, often in a higgledy-piggledy extension built to replace the original

outside toilet. Increasing the size of the house any further to house a new kitchen and laundry appliances was out of the question, and therefore everything was squished into the already tiny kitchen. For most families, the kitchen and running of the home was historically the sole domain of the woman, and therefore comfort and spaciousness were not high on the requirement list when the building was altered.

The staggering increase in the cost of houses and flats has pulled our poorly designed homes and shoddily built extensions into sharp focus. This, coupled with increased

globalization, social media, travel and all the inventions of modern life, we now demand more from our homes. A lot more. So how do we start to unpick and solve the common design problems in our homes? How do we re-imagine and open up the dark corridors, narrow hallways and tiny cramped kitchens?

 LIVING

 KITCHEN

 DINING

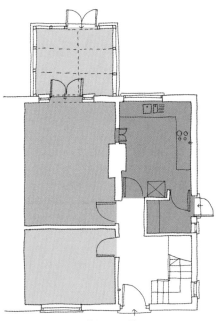

1940s + 1950s

HOMES RAPIDLY BUILT AFTER WORLD WAR II LACK ELEMENTS SUCH AS FEATURE WINDOWS AND FIREPLACES TO SAVE TIME AND MONEY. THE QUALITY OF THE BUILD DETERIORATED.

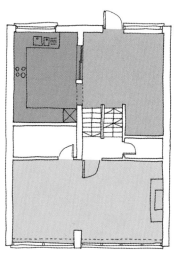

1960s + 1970s

RADICAL SHIFT IN LIVING WITH THE ADVENT OF OPEN- AND SPLIT-PLAN LIVING. AMPLE STORAGE AND BUILT-IN WARDROBES. EXPANSES OF GLAZING AND FEATURE FIREPLACES ARE COMMON.

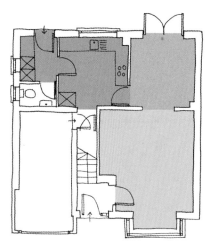

1990s + 2000s

SIMILAR TO THE VICTORIAN LAYOUT, FLOW IS OFTEN ILL-CONSIDERED. ALL ROOMS SEPARATED BY DOORS, FEATURE BAY WINDOWS AND FIREPLACES ARE OFTEN BUILT IN FOR A VICTORIAN LOOK.

Design
solutions

At this point in your home-design journey, you will have a clear idea of how to read plans, and you may have even drawn up your existing layout. You have established your brief and I hope you have a clear idea of what you want to achieve.

So let's close your Pinterest windows, unfollow the sickeningly unobtainable Instagram home accounts and burn all your interiors magazines. Okay, not quite, but it is easy to become so swamped by the fast-fashion interior trends that it can seem impossible to find your own style, or even know where to begin. Although it is great to hold inspirational images in your head, or even at a push in a folder, they are for reference only. Your home is unique to you and your location. We are all accustomed to a simple, square box extension whacked onto the back of a house with little or no thought. But have you ever been in two houses that are absolutely identical? Even contemporary cookie-cutter estate homes cannot physically be in the exact same location, and therefore there is always something slightly different about the views from the windows, how the wind whips around a certain corner and where the sunniest spot is.

THE TEXTURE OF AN UNDECORATED, STRIPPED WALL FORMS A DRAMATIC BACKDROP TO THIS DINING AREA.

In the countless layouts I have created over the years, I have never produced a carbon-copy design of a project – even for seemingly identical homes. I do not have a book of side-return templates for Victorian flats, or loft conversions for 1930s houses. What is the same every time, however, is the line of questioning and design methodology. How and where I start to look and tackle the issues, what to ask and, most importantly, when to listen. It is all about what to ask yourself and what to expect of your home. The route to the design is always the same for me, yet the outcome is as varied and unique as snowflakes falling on a winter's day. Sounds pretty clichéd I know, but it's true.

My initial line of questioning is always the same 'how do you live your life?'. Though it sounds both completely trivial and impossibly all-encompassing at the same time, when you break the question down it becomes much more tangible. From waking up in the morning to going to sleep at night, breaking down your day-to-day life in terms of meals is the most logical and universal place to start. Whether it's a hastily eaten bowl of cornflakes while checking emails at 6am, a regular family evening meal, fasting during Ramadan or an extended family weekend feast. Do you live for your summer barbecues and cocktail evenings, or is it critical for you to keep a Kosher or vegan

kitchen? Breaking down your day and week around food will give you an easy 'in' to see where your home and its layout is not working with you, but fighting against you.

If you aspire to eating at the dinner table every evening but rarely achieve it, why is that? If you want to entertain family and friends but hate it because you end up locked away in the kitchen, how do you make a change to facilitate a more cohesive layout? If your breakfast is a juggle of stress and toast rather than a peaceful moment sitting bathed in sunshine, how do you go about allowing the natural easterly early morning light into your home? How can you visually or physically separate spaces that have more than one use during the day? Where can we start to look to carve out a space for home working so we can separate it from the dining table?

Getting started on design can be daunting, and just working out where to even begin can often feel like an insurmountable task. This chapter breaks down the process of design into three key elements, and by demystifying what seems like design sorcery, you will start to see how your needs and wants can shape your proposed layout.

My three design rules

WE CAN BREAK DOWN THE THREE
DESIGN RULES IN THE PLAN:

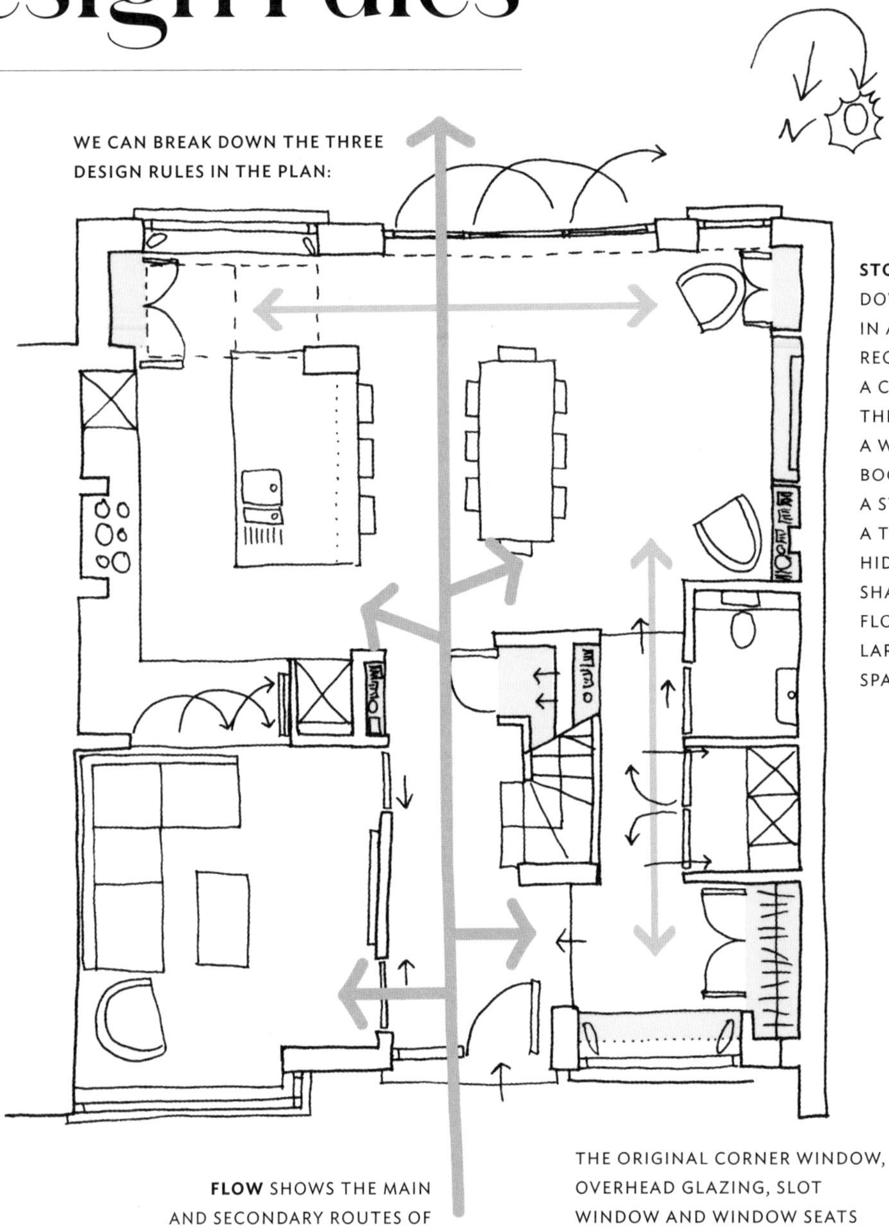

STORAGE IS BROKEN
DOWN AND DISTRIBUTED
IN AREAS WHERE IT IS
REQUIRED:
A COAT STORE AT
THE ENTRANCE WITH
A WINDOW SEAT,
BOOKSHELVES,
A STORAGE WALL WITH
A TV THAT CAN BE
HIDDEN AWAY, AND
SHALLOW BUT WIDE
FLOOR-TO-CEILING
LARDER CUPBOARD
SPACES.

FLOW SHOWS THE MAIN
AND SECONDARY ROUTES OF
CIRCULATION AND VISUAL LINKS
BETWEEN THE SPACES.

THE ORIGINAL CORNER WINDOW,
OVERHEAD GLAZING, SLOT
WINDOW AND WINDOW SEATS
CREATE LIGHT AND ZONES
WITHIN THE SPACE.

There are infinite ways that homes can be designed and redesigned – open-plan, broken-plan, closed-plan, even no-plan. The variety and diversity of layouts and ideas can be mind-boggling, especially when flicking through gorgeous interiors magazines. Breaking down layout types and design ideas into clear categories allows you to identify what you can use and where you can use it. This groundwork will enable you to start unpicking the problem areas and creating the solutions to them.

I really love to work in-plan. In fact, having a layout drawing in front of me is the only way I can start working on a design. Seeing how all the spaces are set out and how they interconnect is not something I can visualize; I need to see it on paper. However, once in the plan I can see everything: the effect that opening up a wall would have in terms of allowing in sunlight, the kind of space that would be created if a door was widened, or where to squeeze in practical storage to bring the design together.

The way I work has led directly to me writing this book and, having brought my initial home consultation process online over the last two years, I have naturally distilled my approach to compensate for being able to work on-site. Completely unintentionally

I have created a thorough and systematic approach to home design, one that can be used as a template to understand common design problems but, most importantly, be the framework to create a home layout that is unique to your needs and your home. It is not a series of templates for you to cut, paste and edit to make them fit your needs, it is an inside track into my thought process that will allow you to tackle your home head-on, either on your own or with a designer or architect.

The basic requirement for our homes is that – with varying levels of priority – there are areas for sleeping, cooking, bathing, relaxing and working. It is these, the general basics of domestic design, that allow the strategies in this book to be applied universally, without any concern that a design template will be replicated, despite the vast array of houses and flats. In a way, it is more about how you think about design. By removing yourself from the reality of day-to-day life, the daily chores such as whether it is the recycling or the refuse bins that need to go out on any given morning, you will start to see your home as an abstract puzzle, and this book will give you the method to begin to solve it. As I have said previously, it isn't intended to replace working with a trained

architect or technician, but the next chapters allow you to break down how you live now, or how you would like to live, and draw the design solution for your home.

Simplification is at the heart of design. If something is simple, it will work seamlessly and efficiently. Getting your home to reflect the essence of who you are can take time, but getting the bones of your design right can bring pleasure and ease into your life for years to come.

Let's look at the core principles that will guide you through the next stages of design. By now, you will have a good idea of your home as it is now, how it looks, its history and the elements that can or cannot be altered. You will have drawn a to-scale plan and, along with a healthy pile of fresh tracing paper and some pens, can start to sketch over the existing layout as I guide you through each step of the way. As mentioned, over the years, I have formed a clear methodology to tackle home design, and the next chapters will help you to shape your space. Here is my blueprint for you, my Three Design Rules to every project I tackle, whether it is small or large, a whole house or an individual room. And they are simplicity itself.

Flow...

...is both the line of sight as you walk through your entrance and the ease with which you move through the space.

Light...

...is where and how the space is lit, whether it's natural light coming in or warm artificial lighting.

Storage...

...eases the transition in through and out of the front door, for each room and each activity, holding or hiding everything from jackets and buggies, clothes and cornflakes, to shoes and tennis rackets, with everything in its place.

These three design standards will allow you to break down and analyze even the most complex design problems to show a clear and intuitive way forward. You may feel that you are going over and over the same problem, but that is a good thing. Sometimes I will find myself spending an inordinate amount of time on one element, such as how the window and doors are set out in a kitchen. You do not have to be content with your first ideas, keep going until you have designed every niggle out of your layout and you feel that there are no compromises remaining in your floor plan. This process leads to the simplification of your design, and it gets to the essence of reflecting your lifestyle within your four, or more, walls.

It was Dieter Rams, the German industrial designer who stated: 'Good design is as little design as possible.' He went on to say: 'Less but better – because it concentrates on the essential aspects, and the products are not burdened with non-essentials. Back to purity, back to simplicity.'

I am definitely on his side. Sometimes, when I have been sketching over and over before finalizing a scheme, I realize it is really quite simple, too simple, too easy, anyone could have come up with it. But then I stand back, have a coffee and pore through some Rams design classics and reassert that actually my scheme is, in fact, great.

These rules can be used for any size of space, from a complete house down to a bedroom or kitchen-dining room. It sounds almost too easy, but when you think about it, the main crunch points in our homes are down to dark, cramped, awkwardly laid out designs, and extensions that have been badly or cheaply built (I think there is a vast difference between cheap and inexpensive). These three design keys address all of these problems.

Dreary corridors with seemingly endless doors? You need **FLOW**.

Dark, uninspired space? Let there be **LIGHT**.

Disorganized and untidy? It's all about **STORAGE**.

Sadly, putting these concepts into a design isn't as simple as drawing a few lines on a plan to create a great layout. As I dissect and put these three simple rules into practice, you will see that they overlap, intertwine and merge into one another. Behind the '…as little design as possible' rule, there are hours and hours of drawing, sketching, redrawing and over sketching until we get there. That, for me, is the process of design. Your drawings will start off messy, fuzzy and unfinished with ink smudges all over your paper and hands, but as you start to tease out the design ideas, the solution will begin to pull in to sharp focus. It is an incredible feeling. It sounds contrived, but I still get excited when an idea that solves the problem and creates a beautiful space in an elegant yet simple architectural move comes together.

So, let's get stuck into how we can shape and form your home, and start our journey through design. I want to begin by breaking down my three design rules so we can see how all-encompassing they are, and how my methodology will work for you and translate into creating your own home design concept.

Flow
Circulation in your home

Flow is one of the most important parts of the design process. It is circulation, it is what you see and it connects you to your space. Flow is the start of absolutely everything in home design. So let's go a little bit deeper into the impact and affect on creating flow in your scheme.

There are two types of circulation to think about: linear and circular. Linear is straight lines and circular is just that, a route that essentially loops in part or in full.

Use a marker pen to draw the routes that you take every day onto your existing plan. Visualize yourself walking in from the front door and putting your stuff away, from the bedroom to the bathroom, from the kitchen to the dinner table, from the living room to the loo, from the bedroom to the washing machine. Establishing how you navigate your home using colourful lines quickly allows you to see the excess circulation, unused areas and wasted space. How this wasted space is incorporated into a design or extension is key. For me, it always starts with simplifying your circulation to the clearest, most simple line possible.

When you begin to analyze the spaghetti-like circulation in your home, and draw in your furniture and fittings, you will quickly see where your most common routes bisect sofas,

tables and kitchen units. You may realize every day that it's annoying when someone walks past the TV when you are engrossed in a film, but until you see it in black and white and marker pen, it is hard to work out what can be done about it. By visualizing the criss-crossing routes that cut a room into two parts, or having a sofa or dining table slap bang in the middle of your circulation, you can start to see the pinch points and how little free space is left over. It is a universal truth that even the biggest homes or largest rooms feel small and cramped when the circulation is confused and erratic.

Destination spaces like sitting rooms may benefit from eliminating circulation that cuts through the main floor area. If there is more than one entrance, keeping the openings as close together as possible ensures the maximum amount of uninterrupted space in the room. Although it is not always possible, having a view through into your living space is a simple way to organize the space as you walk through your home.

So, a view through your home does not always mean outside to a garden or outdoor space, and for many of us in flats or houses opening up long linear vistas is not always possible. Layering your view is key.

CREATING A VIEW + LAYERING

Consider how to create and curate a view. Start by looking at a blank wall then think about what is on the other side.

AN OUTSIDE WALL

If it is an outside wall, then a window is the most obvious idea. Where possible, lowering and extending a windowsill can turn an ordinary window into a window seat that will not only give light and a view, but seating and even storage.

A FLAT WALL

Where forming a window is not possible – maybe the other side of the wall is your neighbour's living room – then create focus here. A flat wall can become the simple background for an oversized picture or mirror. You can also build the wall out to create additional storage, using bookshelves and lighting to give a focus to a previously unexciting wall.

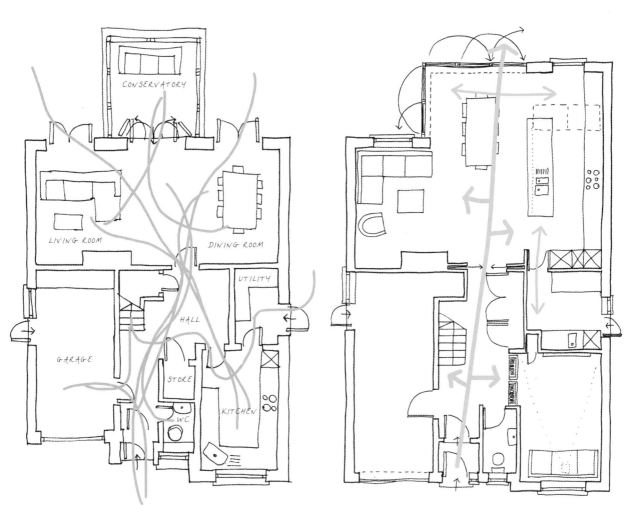

CONSERVATORY

LIVING ROOM

DINING ROOM

UTILITY

HALL

GARAGE

STORE

WC

KITCHEN

DRAWING THE LINES OF CIRCULATION
ONTO THE EXISTING LAYOUT CLEARLY
SHOWS THE CHAOS AND DISORDER OF
THE EXISTING CIRCULATION. THE NEW
DESIGN SHOWS THE RATIONALIZATION
AND SIMPLIFICATION OF THE FLOW.

Making an entrance

What you see and how you feel when you walk through the door into your own space, whether it is rented or owned, is hugely important. Arriving home should be effortless, whether you're alone or piled high with bags, and the way you are able to greet guests is also paramount. It is the entrance to your home and symbolic of how the rest of your space comes together. There is evidence that stress levels are increased when we are surrounded by clutter. (Full disclosure, my entrance hall is often cluttered and disorganized.) I want to look at why the entrance hall can feel like a stopping point rather than a starting one, and how some typical layouts can make you feel hemmed in even if there is no actual clutter.

We are going to look at and implement the three key elements of **FLOW**, **LIGHT** and, of course, **STORAGE**. How you combine these points depends on your unique space and your needs, but following them will allow you to create a seamless, elegant yet functional entrance.

This will help you to not only unlock the drama of your home but it will also signal your style as soon as you open the front door. Look at your plan as if you were walking in through the front door. We know where the north point is, and from that we can ascertain a basic path of the sun, so by rotating your floor plan you can see what is in front of you and how to start to find the flow of your home.

A straight view from your front door to the back of your home is not always possible (it rarely is in flats or converted properties). But that does not mean that we can abandon this principal. In fact, the rule must work harder.

I like to imagine flow as the spine through a layout that connects every space and area. Sometimes it is like the spine of a book, with the pages folding open. Other times it is more complex, perhaps it is offset by a view that creates the link where a direct route is not possible.

I always like to work with straight lines, even when working with a circular design concept. There is an order and flow about a straight line in architectural design that you cannot beat. The other bonus is, it is a structural engineer's dream. Straight lines do not need to mean a long corridor or long thin rooms. Think in terms of views through your home and a straight line punctuated with pools of light. The different living areas in your home come off the line and are clear to access and flow through. Seeing elements such as the dining table and chairs, or a glimpse of glamorous bar stools, allows for easy navigation to the heart of the home no matter how big or small it is. Visualize what you see at the end of your

IN A CONVERTED BASEMENT FLAT WHERE NO EXTERNAL VIEW IS POSSIBLE, A LINEAR VIEW WITH FLOATING SHELVES SHOWS FLOW AND BUILDS IN A FOCUS.

simplified circulation; perhaps it is a view of your outdoor space framed by a glazed door or picture window.

Enlarged areas or openings can form boot rooms, entrance halls, lobbies and stairwells as well as giving opportunities for double height drama, natural light as well as breaking up any feeling of a corridor.

There are many ways to include enlarged openings in your layout, but there are some key details to remember. If your redesigned hallway is the same width as your proposed double doors, then ensure you have enough room for the opened door leaves to sit comfortably against the perpendicular hall walls, and do not position a light switch or socket in the area where the open door will sit.

Double doors are a simple and convenient way to create a grander opening between a hall and a living space. Adding drama and a feeling of space, they look incredible in nearly every house type. One thing to avoid is leaving your opened double doors to swing free in the middle of the room, exacerbating the feeling of a lack of space and looking like a bit of an afterthought rather than a really considered design solution. Think about the location, type and width of your doors and opening. A standard double opening of 1200 mm (47.2 in.) gives a comfortable single door access when the double doors are closed.

If placing a double door on a straight wall, use parliament hinges and allow space on each side of the opening so that when opened, the door leaves can fold back 180 degrees and sit against the wall. Positioning double doors within a thickened bookcase or coat cupboards allow them to sit open discretely yet gives the huge benefit of increased storage, hiding existing walls and even drainage pipes and the structure within.

The style of your interior can be reflected in your doors. Where possible I like to use reclaimed doors from the era of a home. Glazed, textured or simple plain painted doors add style and personality to a space.

Doors can also be designed to sit into pockets in your walls, so they disappear completely when open. The possibilities are endless, and how they can change a space is often underestimated.

EVEN IN A BEAUTIFULLY PROPORTIONED ENTRANCE HALL, BACK, STORE OR TOILET, DOORS CAN DISRUPT THE INITIAL VIEW. HERE, THE STORE DOOR IS DISGUISED AS A OVERSIZED PICTURE FRAME, COMPLETE WITH A HIDDEN CAT FLAP.

Opening up

When your focus is pulled toward a standard, single door, it is not always the most inspiring view, especially if that door just leads to the loo. However, double doors are a different animal altogether. I often like to hide single doors away; I love to make a feature of double doors. They create a real statement and, due to their width, create a feeling of depth in even the narrowest of spaces, or a feeling of openness for the longest corridors.

In the 1990s double doors had a bit of a resurgence in home design. But, unless they are fully closed, they often tend to flap around and get in the way. The key with designing dramatic yet practical double doors is to ensure that the opened door leaves have somewhere to sit when open.

Whether you have reclaimed, reused or even sleek contemporary doors, the opened doors will become part of your overall design. Double doors work well in entrance halls, providing a real focus and style intention to living rooms in a house or flat, but also to more private spaces such as bedrooms and bathrooms, giving a sense of hotel-like opulence when you fling them open to see a beautiful statement bathtub. The extra width also gives a great view out of the bedroom, bathroom or living space, whether that is letting light in from a different aspect or by lining up with a window and a view out.

If you desire the width of a double opening, but not the impact of exposed double doors, or you do not want to loose the wall area needed, then sliding them back into a hidden pocket is a great way to create a seamless, minimal style. The wall itself can open up, or the pocket doors can be at either end. This will leave a section of wall dividing two spaces such as a living room and a dining space that will allow free movement between the two areas, but give visual separation as well as usable floor area if space is at a premium.

Whether your doors are single or double opening, internal bifolding, extra wide sliding panels, steel-framed, timber-glazed, library wall, oversized picture, or hidden, they can completely change the feel of a space, allowing rooms to open up or close down effortlessly.

SINGLE DOORS USUALLY OPEN ONTO AN INDIVIDUAL ROOM.

SETTING THE WALL BACK MAKES THE DOORS LESS OBVIOUS AND ADDS STORAGE SPACE.

BACK-TO-BACK STORAGE IS AN EFFICIENT WAY TO USE SPACE.

FURTHER OPEN UP A SET-BACK WALL TO MAKE IT A FEATURE, MIRROR OR GALLERY WALL.

WHEN A FRONT ROOM DOOR OPENS INWARD, CIRCULATION WILL CROSS DIAGONALLY.

USING DOUBLE DOORS REMOVES THE DIAGONAL ROUTE AND A FIREPLACE BECOMES A FOCUS.

THE ROOM CAN ALSO BE OPENED UP TO INCREASE ITS SIZE.

REDUCE THE PROPORTIONS OF A LONG THIN ROOM USING STORAGE WITH DOUBLE DOORS THAT STAY OPEN TO LINK THE SPACES.

DOUBLE DOORS SIT
AGAINST THE WALLS OF
THIS ENTRANCE HALL,
CREATING A VIEW AND
FLOW AS YOU WALK
THROUGH THE HOUSE.

FLOOR-TO-CEILING HIGH SLIDING PANELS OR DOORS CAN
TRANSFORM A LAYOUT SEAMLESSLY, CREATING SEPARATE
SPACES WITHIN THE FLOW OF YOUR LAYOUT.

THE REMODELLING OF THIS FLAT
INCLUDED THE RELOCATION OF
REDUNDANT CUPBOARD DOORS TO
CREATE DRAMATIC DOUBLE DOORS.
PARLIAMENT HINGES WERE USED AS
THEY ALLOW THE DOORS TO FOLD
OUT OF THE WAY WHEN OPEN.

Vertical circulation: the staircase

You may or may not know it, but I have a slight fixation with stairs. Okay, I am a complete stair obsessive. For me, moving the stairs is often the key to opening up a plan, creating space, allowing natural light to flood in and frame the internal views through a house.

More often than not, the stairs are the first thing you see when you walk into your home. If you live in a house over two or more floors, or you access your flat through a communal hallway, the stairs are one of the most dominant elements of your floor plan.

Stairs are seen by many as an immovable object. If you look at the construction of a flight of stairs, there is a huge amount of void space underneath them. This should be a great storage space, but it is often impossible to access. There are fantastic carpentry and joinery ideas designed to utilize this area. Storage racks that can be pulled out into your hall space and easily accessed from either side can maximize the use of space under the stairs for day-to-day items like shoes or bags.

We are going to look at what amazing things your stairs can become, rather than a large bulky imposition blocking light and limiting flow. They are not just vertical circulation: stairs are everything.

Stairs are usually placed off the main circulation spine. Working with them, opening them up to create a light well above, can be an effective way to bring natural light into the middle of your floor plan.

CREATING A STAIRCASE THAT WRAPS AROUND TO FORM A C-SHAPE PRODUCES A VOID ABOVE THAT MAKES A DRAMATIC DOUBLE-HEIGHT SPACE AND ENSURES THIS SIMPLE STAIRCASE IS THE REAL FOCUS OF THE ENTRANCE HALL. THE PLACEMENT OF THE STAIR NEEDS TO BE CONSIDERED IN TERMS OF HOW IT SITS WITHIN THE OTHER FLOORS IT ACCESSES, BE THEY UPPER OR LOWER. IF A LOFT CONVERSION IS POSSIBLE IN THE FUTURE, ENSURE THAT THE PROPOSED STAIR DESIGN CAN BE EXTENDED UP THROUGH THE HOUSE WITHOUT HAVING TO BE REDONE IN THE FUTURE.

Limitations + possibilities

I want to look at the limitations and possibilities of a typical domestic staircase. When I am redesigning or extending a house, I often use it as my initial focal point. The stairs are usually positioned around the mid-point of a house plan and are a great place to look to bring height, light and drama into a space.

The key with re-jigging or re-positioning the stairs is to think in terms of the bottom and top step of your flight, as well as how it works on each level. A straight run is the most common form of staircase, either with a straight, simple turn, winder or landing as the last few steps to the floor above. If you think about how you come downstairs in the morning, typically you are looking at your front door with no real cushion or buffer between the bottom step and the outside world. In a typical stair layout with a pitch roof above, there is often a small window, allowing for a little bit of borrowed light on the staircase.

A simple, small yet hugely effective alteration to your existing stairs is to turn the bottom of the last few steps. Incorporating a simple winder turn here can provide several opportunities. Depending on your layout, this creates a usable zone between your front door and the stairs that can be utilized for coat and shoe storage – from simple hooks and a shelf, to seating, fitted storage or making room for a specific item such as a vintage hall stand.

Coming down more centrally in the layout means more efficient circulation and gives you the opportunity to land opposite a new opening in a wall. You can create a view looking through some lovely big double doors to your dining room or living space. Think about the layers. Maybe there is a fireplace in the room opposite that you can frame; or a glimpse of beautifully curated, or even really, messy shelving; or maybe a great big cheese plant as you walk past. Creating flow and drama using even these little things, can enable a small move to create huge possibilities.

A turn can make the stair void above wider, creating the effect of a double-height space and maximizing any light from a window or skylights above. In typical 1930s, 1940s and 1950s homes, a simple winding turn at the top of the stairs can often free up landing space from a straight run to give storage the depth of the stair itself. This lends itself brilliantly to a utility space, with drainage conveniently already there in the adjacent bathroom.

In many Victorian layouts, the head of the stairs can be turned more efficiently to give extra floor area to that outrigger room that is commonly a few steps below the main floor level.

ALTHOUGH NOT THE MOST SPACE EFFICIENT CHOICE IN A COMPACT LAYOUT, IF YOU HAVE ROOM, A SPIRAL STAIRCASE CAN BECOME A STRIKING, SCULPTURAL FEATURE INTEGRATING NATURAL LIGHT FROM ABOVE.

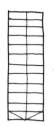

STRAIGHT STAIR RUN

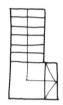

LANDING STEP TO TOP
OF STRAIGHT RUN

L-SHAPED STAIR
WITH WINDERS

C-SHAPED STAIR WITH
MID-LANDING
OR STEPPED MID-LANDING

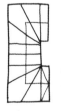

WINDERS AT THE TOP
AND BOTTOM STEPS

ALTERNATE
TREAD STEPS FOR
SPACE EFFICIENCY

SPIRAL STAIRCASE

ALWAYS LOOK FOR OPPORTUNITIES
TO INCORPORATE LIGHT AND DESIGN
ELEMENTS IN YOUR STAIRCASE. EVEN
THE SIMPLEST OF STAIRS CAN BECOME
A FOCUS OF THE SPACE AND A FUN
WAY TO INCORPORATE STORAGE
AND DISPLAY.

Light
Letting the sun in

Sunlight is a crucial factor when designing any home or space. Maximizing natural light cannot be underestimated. Houses and flats, even seemingly identical terraced houses, are never exactly the same. On top of that, how we live is so completely different whether we have a big family, a small family, are a single person with a big dog or a couple with a small cat – we all need different things from our homes. So, you can see, before we even touch on aspect, sunlight and location, a standard box extension to the maximum permitted size dotted with a row of skylights and spotlights cannot possibly solve your wide variety of complex needs.

In order to orientate myself within a plan, the first thing I do is to find the property on a satellite photograph to identify which way is north. This allows me to sketch the path of the sun from east to west, as described in Establishing a brief (see page 38).

NORTH LIGHT

North light is considered quite flat and cool; it rarely changes and so it can give a beautiful and constant level of brightness. Due to the lack of direct sunlight, walls and windows facing north can be cold and externally prone to damp and moss. Art galleries, studios, sports halls and manufacturing buildings favour this lighting. Think of the ubiquitous sawtooth factory roof with triangular windows like teeth that give a constant, cool light to the occupants or machinery below. This north-facing roof glazing was first developed for weaving mills during the Industrial Revolution in northern England in the early to mid-1800s.

EAST LIGHT

Early morning light flooding in from the east casts beautiful long shadows and is clean and rich in feel. It is said that east light is the best light for dressing and putting on your make-up, if you are that way inclined. There is something quite energizing about it and, for obvious reasons, it works incredibly well in the spaces where you can bring that morning glow into your kitchen or breakfast area.

SOUTH LIGHT

We are all conditioned to think that a south-facing aspect is great for a living space. I am not quite so sure. Although I love the intensity of light from the south, it can quickly overheat a space and be far too, well, light. And when it floods onto your television screen you may find that you always have the blinds or curtains closed in order to see the screen.

WEST LIGHT

This warm amber light always makes me think of summer, and bringing it into living and dining spaces works beautifully. If you are lucky enough to be able to see the sun setting from certain parts of your home at certain times of the year, then be sure to frame this with a stunning picture window that will also look fabulous on a dreary drizzly day or in the depths of winter.

By noticing the differences between direct light coming in from due south, clear early morning easterly sunlight or the warm fire-like glow of the evening sun coming in from the west, we can start to rationalize our living spaces according to aspect. Locating rooms where it does not matter if artificial light is used, such as toilets and utility spaces in north-facing parts of your home, can open up the plan to create living spaces in the naturally lit areas.

Once you have drawn the path of the sun onto your plan – I always like to draw a small sun for good measure – it will be easy to see where the sunniest and shadiest parts of your home are. You will clearly be able to see from your simple diagram where the sunniest and shadiest parts of your home are. These are the rooms to avoid arranging around the sunniest or most lovely parts of the house layout where possible. On the flip side, dark areas work brilliantly for cosy spaces and rooms. Imagine a cold, north-facing window with no direct sunlight that benefits from an incredible view out over a garden, tree or streetscape. Relegating this space to a closed-off toilet or shoe cupboard would mean that stunning view is lost, therefore it is so important to know what you are looking for when you read a plan.

Not every house or flat enjoys a south-facing aspect, and therefore it is vital to understand the rules and thought process of aspect in order to apply it to your own space. For example, how and where can you get direct south light into your living space if it faces north?

A SECTION SHOWING THE SAWTOOTH ROOF STRUCTURE THAT GIVES SCOOPS OF INDIRECT LIGHT TO THE LIVING SPACES BELOW.

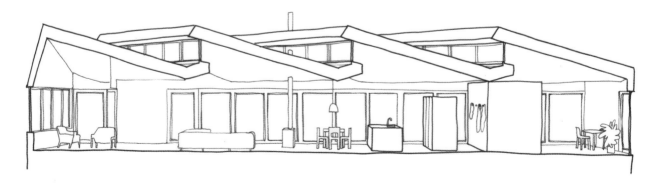

Glazing + windows

I sometimes think that when an architect mentions 'glazing' it summons visions of huge sheets of frameless glass being craned in place to form a minimal glazed box and the expense that it entails. For me, glazing is not always about an endless expanse of glass, it is all about first impressions.

There are so many terms and descriptions for windows, which I think reflects (no pun intended) their wide number of uses within the home. Fenestration, glazing, lights, glass, bay, oriel, casement, picture, frameless... the list seems endless, and the importance of getting your windows right cannot be understated.

Windows are not simply for light in and views out of a home. The look and style of your glazing is one of the main drivers of your home's aesthetic. Minimal or traditional, the material and proportions of your windows are key to your overall design. You will be amazed at the impact that lowering

the often painfully high windowsills of mid- to late 20th century houses and flats can achieve to create a more balanced elevation.

During the initial design process, think about the view of your home as you approach it as much as you do the internal layout. It is sometimes handy to locate a downstairs toilet near the front door, but be mindful of other spaces, such as bathrooms and ensuite shower rooms close by. If rooms that require obscure, frosted or privacy glass are loaded onto the front elevation, it can make a home look uninviting. When it comes to utility and boot rooms, think about how you use the space within the room with respect to any visible window. A sink with cleaning products and bleach bottles stacked against the window is not an overly attractive look as you walk up to your front door. I like to locate family bathrooms, loos and ensuite bath and shower

LOWERING WINDOWSILLS AND ALTERING THE PROPORTIONS OF THE WINDOWS ACROSS A WHOLE ELEVATION IS AN EASY UPDATE THAT AVOIDS THE EXPENSE OF ANY STRUCTURAL CHANGES TO THE LINTELS ABOVE.

rooms internally if possible, rather than allowing permanently obscured glass to hide the views. I know an internal loo does not suit everyone, but if you imagine a glamorous hotel bathroom, add in an effective vortex extraction fan and even a high level rooflight where possible, and then your windows can be dedicated to rooms where light, relaxing and views are more critical.

When you are starting to zone the areas of your layout, think about how you use the rooms in your home as well as the aspect. The enjoyment of the crisp, early morning easterly light can be short-lived. On long summer days, unless you are up at 5am for yoga, work or small children, you will probably miss those first hours after sunrise. Whereas on a day off, the afternoon and evening light from the west feels like it can last until you jump into bed. In the winter months, even a glimpse of the low, reddish sun can fill your heart with joy. By anticipating this, including it in your brief and then in your drawn design, you will bring in that opportunity rather than have it in your home by happy coincidence.

Just like framing a view with a window, you can track the path of the sun or frame certain positions to create direct or indirect light, or even projections or reflections of the sunshine in your home.

If you have directly south-facing windows or skylights, over-heating can be a real problem during the summer months. On the flipside, the further you are away from the equator, this added warmth is often a welcome addition. Apart from on the hottest of hot summer's days, due-north facing elevations can be unfathomably cold. Therefore proposing a large wall-sized glazed opening here would be a mistake. Equally, if you are proposing expanses of glass in a south-facing room, there are a few ways to mitigate the overheating of your space.

If you want to embrace seamless glazing, then one option, albeit quite an expensive one, is to go down the highly insulated, solar-coated, triple-glazing route. This high-tech solution can vastly reduce heat and glare where needed. But, you know me, I love a passive and cost-effective solution and prefer to design in ways to reduce the impact of the sun's heat. Breaking up south-facing glazing with stone or brick can help to absorb and dissipate solar gain, from the classic 'orangery' style to a contemporary design that breaks up your façade to create picture windows and slot glazing and give views in and out without baking the occupants. Where glazing is reduced, light can still be introduced through the ceiling. Rather than facing south, angling your roof glazing to face north, east or west will create a wash of light

THIS SECTION OF A
SOUTH-FACING HOUSE
SHOWS HOW A SLATTED
PERGOLA REDUCES
SOLAR GAIN AND, WITH
ADDITIONAL PLANTING,
PROMOTES COOLING. IT
HAS THE ADDED BENEFIT
OF BRINGING THE
OUTSIDE IN.

that will change throughout the day
and the seasons.

Any large expanses of glazing that
experience intense periods of sun can
be shaded with a pergola or *brise soleil*
that can also become the framework
for bringing planting into your design.

You can use glazing to enhance
the feeling of space in more cramped
or challenging of spaces. In loft
conversions, where head height is
lowered for example, look to maximize
the opportunities that working with
your roof space can bring. When you
are designing your access or stairs to
the new top-floor space, drama can be
brought to the narrowest of stairwells
by opening up to the roofline above
and installing long slit skylights. With
smaller spaces, design an oversized
skylight to play with the proportion
of the room and flood it with light.
Linking the stairwell down to the
ground floor can give a wonderful
double- or triple-height space.

Where you do not have the
convenience of a standard room shape,
you need to think about the glazing

details a little differently. Rather than
a typical bulky casement window with
a standard height windowsill, if you
opt for a slim-framed fixed pane you
can lower the windowsill to form a
window seat. Lowering the windowsill
further to the floor will give a
beautiful, simple picture window that
will become the focus of the space.
You look past the awkward proportions
of the room to the view out. Always
remember that when you lower a
windowsill below the standard height
of 800 mm (31.4 in.), you must use
toughened glass just as you would with
glazed doors to conform to building
regulations. Moving away from
conventional window types will give
impact and drama in a space where it
may otherwise feel a little cramped.

A tip for giving the feeling of
bespoke glazing on a budget, is to
look up the different sizes of off-the-
shelf roof windows and skylights.
You will be surprised at the array
of sizes and proportions you can
buy without having to go down the
bespoke glazing route.

If you want to install a dormer window, or renovate an existing one, think about glazing the cheeks of your dormer as well as the usual outward-facing window. This additional side glazing will give a panoramic view and allow natural light in all the way around. The movement of the sun throughout the day, coupled with the almost uninterrupted view out, will draw the focus of the room. Where angles dominate a space, let them shine through. Emphasize the outline of sharp corners and awkward wall junctions by creating geometric patterns using paint and wallpaper and the ceiling will become seamlessly integrated into the design. Alternatively, these angles can be softened with draped fabrics and floor-to-ceiling curtains can frame a view.

The other thing that glazing can do is join elements of your build together. Combine that with using your aspect to your advantage, and you can start to introduce light and architectural design into your home.

If you are planning a single-storey extension, you will often find that your existing ceiling height will not match your proposed build. Homes built before the home-building boom after World War II often enjoy ceiling heights of nearly 3 m. Contemporary planning regulations will restrict the final height of your build, therefore a common design problem is how to seamlessly connect the lower ceiling levels of your proposed build with those in your original home. How do you achieve the balance of beauty, elegance and budget? There are many ways to eliminate that step down without creating a bulkhead or huge beam oppressively hanging down and glass is the perfect solution. By stopping the new ceiling and the original house short, you create a gap between the two elements. This crack of light is a perfect and cost-effective way to join old and new and we will cover using skylights as a way to bring spaces together in more detail in the next chapter.

THIS SECTION OF A HOUSE SHOWS THE FEELING OF DOUBLE HEIGHT SPACE CREATED BY A RAKED CEILING AND ROOF GLAZING ABOVE A STAIRWELL.

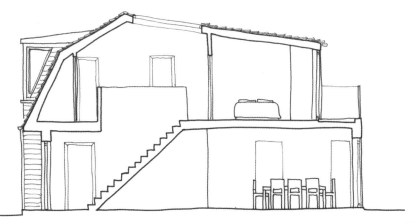

THE KITCHEN WORKTOP EXTENDS INTO THE WINDOW TO GIVE EXTRA SPACE AND INCREASE THE LIGHT.

A CONVEX MIRROR BOUNCES LIGHT AROUND THE ROOM AND ILLUMINATES A DARK INTERIOR SCHEME.

ADDING GLAZING TO THE CHEEK OF A DORMER WINDOW GIVES A PANORAMIC VIEW FROM THE FIRST FLOOR AND INCREASES THE FLOOR AREA. THE SOUTH-FACING GLAZING IS SPLIT TO ALLOW IN LIGHT AND PASSIVE SOLAR HEATING, WITHOUT OVERHEATING THE SPACES WITHIN.

Directing the light

THE SKYLIGHT OVER A
FLOOR-TO-CEILING PICTURE
WINDOW PROVIDES A COST-
EFFECTIVE WAY OF CREATING
UP-AND-OVER GLAZING. IT
ALSO GIVES VIEWS OUT AND
UP, AND ALLOWS YOU TO
STARGAZE AT NIGHT.

HIGH LEVEL SLOT GLAZING
BRINGS LIGHT DEEP INTO
THE PLAN AND JOINS
THE DIFFERING CEILING
HEIGHTS OF THE EXISTING
HOME AND EXTENSION
TOGETHER ELEGANTLY.

Incorporating a south-facing window into a plan is a great idea if you do not have one already. One of my beloved tricks is to create a pop-out extension with a glazed door or window perpendicular to the main wall. This effectively creates a courtyard, opening up and introducing a new aspect of light into your home. It will give all the benefits of the intense, southerly light that moves with the path of the sun, without the associated over-heating or glare. Rather than reorienting the whole house, or just the living room, to face the south, you can create little pockets of southerly light and use them to highlight different areas. When these tricks of the light are coupled with layering your view – which we will come to next – the overall effect can be incredibly elegant and dramatic, and the ever-changing light will bring a real sense of joy to your home.

Other ways to bring the light in, rather than a high strip window or a clerestory (see page 101) is to think about other ways to introduce a slot window. A thin, vertical, floor-to-ceiling slice of glass opening, or a slice of glass laid horizontally at floor level, can be a unique way to bring light in without worrying about overlooking or being overlooked.

I know it sounds like a hackneyed trick, but where you cannot extend in any direction to bring in a new aspect of light into your home mirrors can work wonders. If you place a convex mirror so that it reflects direct light back into the home, it will reflect the light in myriad ways, unlike a standard straight mirror. Oversize concave mirrors can be extremely expensive, but try this tip. You can buy a huge acrylic traffic or factory safety mirror and it will pretty much do the same job. They often come with an insipid grey plastic surround, but you can easily use paint or gold or silver leaf to make it look like a stunning contemporary frame. If mixed with vintage mirrors and pictures, no one will ever suspect a thing.

Light
+ drama

Bringing light into your home from above goes hand-in-hand with creating drama. Even the simplest roof light will not only flood your layout with natural light, but will also give a sense of height and a view out that will break up your ceiling line. Where you are connecting to an existing structure, the way the architecture of your extension connects to your home, both in plan section and externally gives a fantastic opportunity for an exciting design that will make the most of your site and help create a unique home that works perfectly for you.

As well as enabling you to move between floors, a staircase is a great opportunity for drama and light if it is treated as a piece of inventive joinery. You can simply modernize existing stairs by replacing the spindles, or go all the way and add bespoke storage below and skylights above.

Creating a light well to your staircase brings drama and natural light down through your room plan. It is common for a flight of stairs to sit against an outside wall and be positioned underneath the junction with your roof. A straightforward, albeit fiddly, way to open up a stairwell is to remove the existing flat ceiling and create a sloped one to your existing roof rafter line. Then you can install skylights to flood the stairwell with light. You can retain the existing roof timbers to create a mini atrium.

When I think of roof glazing, I see blue skies, fluffy clouds and maybe a bird flying overhead. But at night, skylights can appear like a black hole, unless artificial lighting is used to create a reflection back into your home.

Understanding the aspect of your home is important too. Large expanses of south-facing glazing can quickly overheat the room below, or predominantly north-facing glazing can sometimes feel like it is sucking warmth from the space during the colder months. Think about glazing in terms of articulating areas, connecting spaces as well as throwing light down into a dark area or lighting a wall or zone. Consider how you can close the glazing off to give a feeling of warmth and intimacy in the darker hours. Glazing also joins elements of your build together. Combined with using your aspect to your advantage, you can start to introduce light and architectural design into your home.

TIMBER RAFTERS ARE EXPOSED AND PAINTED. THE HIGH-LEVEL GLAZING SITTING ABOVE THEM HAS SIMPLE, CLEAN LINES AND APPEARS TO BE FRAMELESS.

GLAZING ON THE EXISTING RAKED CEILING COMBINED WITH AN ATRIUM ABOVE CREATES THE APPEARANCE OF A TRIPLE-HEIGHT SPACE.

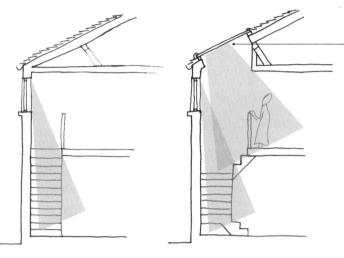

RAKING THE CEILING ABOVE A STAIRCASE FLOODS THE STAIRWELL BELOW WITH LIGHT. TURNING THE TOP AND BOTTOM OF THE STAIRS CREATES TWO WINDERS, INCREASES THE OPENING AND FORMS A MINI DOUBLE HEIGHT SPACE.

STAIRCASES ARE A GREAT PLACE TO INTRODUCE DRAMA AND EXCITEMENT. HERE A DOUBLE-HEIGHT SPACE ABOVE THE ENTRANCE HALL INCLUDES A FEATURE LIGHT FITTING SUSPENDED BETWEEN THE TWO FLOORS. THE NORTH-EAST FACING OVERSIZED PICTURE WINDOW AND SLOT WINDOW BRING EARLY MORNING SUNSHINE INTO THE SPACE AND ENSURE A LIGHT-FILLED ENTRANCE HALL BELOW.

A SLOT OF GLAZING WASHES THE WALL AND THE AREA BELOW IT WITH NATURAL LIGHT.

Storage

Storage is more than just a cupboard. It is a utility room or wardrobe, a larder or even a window seat. Circulation and storage are easy companions, I might even say they are best buddies. Simplifying routes through your home and creating views is about creating flow. One of the beauties of this is the leftover or dead space. Unlike the dead space you identify in your existing floor plan that might house a dusty dresser with a pile of unopened envelopes on it, the left-over space created by your new,

sleek circulation routes can become very purposeful storage. At an entrance it can house coats, bags, buggies and a scooter or two; near the bedrooms it may contain clean linen. Storage that is the size, design and position required to hold what it needs to hold.

Linear circulation routes can easily become a narrow and gloomy corridor. How do you prevent it slipping into that damming category? You must break out of the line visually with light and layering. Where a fabulous view of fields or sky to draw the eye is not

possible, then creating a view within your home is as important as having one out of a window. So this is about finding neat and simple circulation, which means that every single room comes off that singular circulation route so that you are not crossing any of the rooms, maximizing the usable floor space and giving a real feeling of space. Awkward nooks and crannies, electricity meters or even parts of the structure can be hidden behind floor-to-ceiling storage doors to give a feeling of height and a sleek way to hide storage and frame a view through the home, forming a spine wall. Long lengths of shelving give space for artwork, books and unopened post. They also create a really beautiful sense of perspective that enhances the whole vista as your eye looks down. Layering works off to the side of the spine of circulation gives pools of light or openings to get away from the feeling of a corridor.

A NARNIA CUPBOARD OPENS UP SHOWING THE UTILITY ROOM AND DRYING RACK. THE STORAGE AND TOILET ARE TUCKED AWAY AND HIDDEN OUT OF SIGHT.

HIDDEN STORAGE

No matter the size of your home, being able to integrate storage into your space is fundamental. As you look to increase the number of locations and amount of storage, finding ways to disguise it will allow it to flow into your design rather than stand out. Doors that close flush can be decorated with the same paint colour or finish as the wall that they sit in. All that is left is the shadow gap around them, hinting at the location of the storage behind. The doors can be different widths and materials to give a bespoke look.

Panelling, pictures and mirrors can open up to form storage, access or hide away bulky gas and electricity meters, consumer units and odd bits of jutting out wall in an elegant way. Narnia cupboards are my absolute favourite, and a great space-efficient way to hide away areas of storage. They work particularly well in kitchens, where the floor-to-ceiling doors can easily and seamlessly be transformed into an access door.

CENTRAL PANELS DISGUISE THE ACCESS TO A WARDROBE AND ENSUITE SHOWER ROOM.

A NARNIA CUPBOARD DOOR IS NESTLED IN A CORNER, INDISTINGUISHABLE FROM THE LARDER DOORS AND AN INTEGRATED FRIDGE-FREEZER.

THE SAME MATERIAL COVERS THE WALL AND DOORS, SO IT CAN DISAPPEAR OR BECOME AN ELEGANT PIECE OF CARPENTRY, EXPOSING THE RECORDS AND OBJECTS, BUT HIDING AWAY THE CLUTTER.

STORAGE AS DESIGN

Open shelving can give a feeling of depth and interest, breaking up what could start to become a little monotonous. Designing a combination of tucked away storage and open sections where your objects can be displayed can form the focus of a room as well as being highly practical. You can expand on the idea of the library or gallery wall, bringing together the storage of magazines and books with items that express your style. I have never colour-coded my bookshelves or kitchen shelves, but it is an effective way to create a look that you can change and edit as you please.

Walk-through wardrobes maximize the use of space where floor area is limited. Using a minimal depth of hanging space and shallow shelves for shoe or boxed storage doubles up the use of the area, access and storage. In a home working space or office, using a surface-mounted storage base such as a peg board, pigeonholes or clipboards will allow you to create a usable look.

A NARROW WALK-THROUGH WARDROBE GIVES PLENTY OF STORAGE AND DISPLAY, BUT THE FOCUS IS ON THE WALL BEYOND WHICH HAS A PANEL COVERED IN GOLD LEAF AND AN INSET SHELF.

OPEN SHELVES IN KITCHENS ARE A FANTASTIC WAY TO DISPLAY AND ACCESS YOUR TABLEWARE. ALTHOUGH OPEN SHELVING CAN BE A DUST TRAP, IF YOU USE THE ITEMS EVERY DAY THERE IS LITTLE TIME FOR THEM TO GATHER DUST.

Using your space

The whole process of design is like piecing together a complicated jigsaw. Sometimes the pieces fit easily with very little effort, but more often than not it takes a lot of working out.

I do not believe that there are two or three design concepts that can be superimposed on each house type. Even on seemingly identical houses, you cannot simply reuse a proposed layout. The minutiae of every home is always different. They are built in different locations, built by hand and lived in by any of us.

Even if you had a tower block with an identical floor plan and two identical flats above each other, one would still have a very slightly different view, reach of the sun and, most importantly, is inhabited in differing ways by individuals, couples, small or extended families who all require differing things and have varying demands that in turn have an impact on the design.

Often houses were designed and built hundreds of years ago, or are new-build housing based on Victorian or Georgian floor plans. But there will be a definite thread that can be picked up and followed through these layouts, a thread that can weave through and bring order to the Tetris-like minefield of residential architecture.

We now have the design process, and know what to look for when sketching onto the existing plans. Now we must find out how to apply this design methodology to your home, to shape and form your space.

TO MAXIMIZE THE FEELING OF SPACE, THE LIVING AND DINING ZONES ARE TUCKED OFF THE MAIN CIRCULATION OF THE HOUSE AND ARE LIT FROM ABOVE. THERE IS A FRAMED VIEW OF THE GARDEN THROUGH THE SLIDING DOORS AND A SLOT WINDOW.

THE HERITAGE OF YOUR HOME

Whether new build or a 17th-century cottage, looking into the existing layout of your property and understanding how any alterations and extensions have been made is vital. Unpicking this layout will account for odd layouts, the strange location of the bathroom or a horrifying lack of storage.

FLOW

Visualize looking through your home, thinking about what you will see and how you will move through the space. No matter the existing layout, whether your home is on one level, split level, or includes a loft conversion and basement, the objective is to create simple clear circulation for the new design. The main circulation connects all the areas and rooms, and includes vertical access to any planned loft or basement conversions.

Creating and framing views to the outside, where possible, as well as internally will enhance the feeling of flow and movement through your home.

Circulation can be linear or circular. If it must be staggered due to an existing constraint or fixed point, try to maintain visual links where possible. A focus on accessibility and mobility will ensure your design is future-proofed for decades to come, whether it will be your forever home or lived in by other occupants.

LIGHT

Whether artificial or natural, light can zone your space and further enhance the routes through and the areas within it. Think about windows in a slightly different way, raising or lowering the windowsills of existing windows can make a huge difference to the amount of light coming in and the views out, especially in rooms with views to a garden.

Think about how to get natural sunlight in from different aspects to enliven your space with early morning light from the east, or warm light from the west in the afternoon and evening.

Roof glazing does not need to be a uniform row of off-the-shelf skylights. Creating high-level slot glazing can join elements of your design together as well as flood the space with light. Be mindful of solar gain and try to use it to your advantage where possible. Passive heating can be achieved with careful positioning of south- or west-facing glazing to bring in warmth into a cooler, north-facing plan.

Glazing does not necessarily need to break the bank to be extraordinary, whether that is narrow slots, clerestory windows (see page 101) or panoramic glazing in a dormer window. How and where you want to light is key.

STORAGE

Storage is not about square footage; it is about position and usability. When you start to think about the flow of your home and the areas and rooms off it, you will see the incongruity of a jutting out utility room or coat cupboard that has an identical door to your living room and blocks your view of a window. Storage is crucial to every function of the home and should be integrated seamlessly into your layout.

Whether you need extra space in your kitchen to separate food preparation through religious, dietary or lifestyle choices, or have a growing or changing family, think about storage as the vital ancillary spaces that serve each room, not an afterthought in your design.

SHAPING YOUR SPACE

Do not be scared about making mistakes and going back to the drawing board, both figuratively and literally. Shaping your space is just that, a fluid process of moulding, moving, altering your lines of flow and circulation, how and where light enters and how you will use each nook and cranny. Use your plan ideas to visualize walking through the design, from getting up in the morning until falling into bed at night. Keep sketching and drawing until you have a layout that works for you, your family, and your home.

Creating spaces

Finding your style

When we think about a house or flat as a whole, it is not just about the two-dimensional floor plan. How that simple black-and-white drawing translates to actual rooms and spaces is critical. Although I don't want to discuss interior design here, it is important to get a sense of the style you are looking to achieve. Tailoring the **FLOW**, **LIGHT** and **STORAGE** to your needs will give rise to very different overall designs, without the merest thought of what cushion covers or kitchen door colour you want. For example, if you want to create a sleek, ultra-minimal design, then a straight line of flow is the main principal to follow, which in turn, sits well with maximizing storage space behind this line of flow. Alternatively, if you are looking to create a more rustic or maximalist style, then the line of flow works well when it is broken, providing niches and layering with areas for display or seating. If you are working toward dark, inky interiors these work incredibly well with natural light, which seems somewhat counter-intuitive. Dark interiors are elevated by direct sunlight moving around the space, but also look incredible with walls washed with a more constant north light from above. Thinking about the placement of glazing and artificial lighting, and the effect it will have in a room in the day and at night, will ensure you achieve a bespoke look and feel no matter your interior design taste.

FORGET FASHION, THIS IS STYLE

As with anything to do with interior design, pull together a mood board of styles you love. Rip pages from magazines and brochures, remembering that the key is not to try to reproduce an individual scheme, but bring together elements to create your own style. Always get physical samples of products you want to use, and invest in a RAL sample colour chart to ensure each colour and texture enhances one another rather than works against each other.

If you are in two minds about a finish or look you love because you are worried that it will look tacky in a couple of years, then there are a few rules I like to follow. Try to be as authentic as possible. If you are in a property that has never seen a brick, let alone has a brick wall ready to be exposed, then avoid

faux effects such as wallpaper or brick slips. As a style, it will always jar with the architecture and, even though you have wanted it for years, it will never seem quite right.

As with any 'statement' finish or item in your home, research the potential manufacturers and get samples to ensure the quality will reflect your design. Often cheaper imitations can look just that, cheap. I am all for cost efficiency, but sometimes it is important to allocate a chunk of the budget to getting a specific element that will look right and last for years, even decades. Like trends in fashion, if you wait long enough interior trends will come back in again. Although when it comes to Artex plaster, I hope it will never return.

Sculpt your space
using flow, light + storage

We have looked at the concepts of **FLOW, LIGHT** and **STORAGE** as separate, individual elements, but now we will bring them together. Remember there is no such thing as a 'wrong' idea in design, it is just part of the process of getting to the right layout for you. Having said that, if you have got to this stage in the book and still have the door to your toilet opening in full view of your front door, then we will need to have words.

Rather than concentrating on the prescriptive specifics of design styles, think about style as a sliding scale from hiding everything away to exposing it all, from household objects to the fabric of the building itself. By breaking down my **THREE DESIGN PRINCIPLES** we will explore how they can both solve layout problems and create the canvas for your style.

We will look at **FLOW** as it weaves into **LIGHT**, and crosses neatly over to **STORAGE**. It is important to create internal movement through your plan as you walk from one room to the other, between floors, or when coming in through the front door – and the back door if you have one. Light punctuates spaces, can create zones and also can indicate to guests the direction they need to go when they enter, leading them from the entrance to the heart of the home or the entertaining area. Designing a clear route both physically and visually aides guests or homeowners with mobility, visual or hearing impairments, linking spaces together for ease of movement and a sense of connection. Where and how storage comes in, either

incidental space created where walls are altered and built out to hide structure, or really considered storage areas specifically designed for a function such as guest coat storage, muddy boots or a soggy dog also needs to be considered.

One of my favourite things to do is to create a view from the front of your house or flat through to the rear, out to an external space, garden or window. Where this is not possible, you can use your sightlines to bring focus to an internal view that can be as simple as a picture or mirror. It is about creating little glimpses of excitement, and even intrigue, as you get a view all the way through the full extent of the house or flat. This in turn provides an overall feeling of space, no matter the size of your home.

POOLS OF LIGHT FROM THE ROOF LIGHT, CLERESTORY WINDOW AND GLAZED DOORS HIGHLIGHT THE LIVING SPACES THAT ARE JUST OUT OF SIGHT IN THIS VIEW THROUGH THE HOME.

Flow

I often look for one simple move, a master stroke that opens up and solves a lot of issues within an existing layout. Personally, I like to start at the front door and look through the house as if I have just walked in. Don't be afraid of sketching over and over again to mitigate any compromises within your proposed layout. If your front door is currently in an awkward position or under used, look at the effect that moving it has as an initial option. It may be the first step toward solving your design dilemma. In some house types the front door is a real feature. It can be integral to the design and style of the building itself, and maybe neighbouring houses too, therefore I would actively discourage you from moving it in this instance. If moving a less imposing front door is an option, rather than just blocking it up, the original doorway can work well as floor-to-ceiling glazing or a window seat, which will keep an echo of the original elevation.

IN THROUGH THE OUT DOOR

Back doors are often in a slightly awkward position, or take up valuable wall space and be blocked by piles of washing or extra freezer. Maybe your back door is invaluable for access to garden storage, or essential if you have muddy boots, dogs or bikes. Whatever your needs, your design can seek to accommodate them.

Think about both the flow from any additional doors into the main house. Is the back door connected to the entrance hall? Is it a fairly grand door or does it provide a hidden exit through the kitchen? Having direct access from your back door into a larder or pantry space will allow any grocery shopping to be put away directly, without the need to traipse it through the house. If your back door is slightly more utilitarian, then ensuring you have access to put out the recycling is important, or plan your home so you can easily get out via your utility space to hang out the washing to dry.

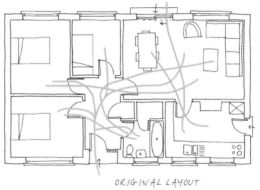

ORIGINAL LAYOUT

IN THE EXISTING LAYOUT OF THIS BUNGALOW THE ENTRANCE OPENS INTO A HALLWAY WHICH LOOKS STRAIGHT AT THE BEDROOM DOORS. THE CIRCULATION MIXES THE PRIVATE BEDROOMS WITH THE PUBLIC LIVING AND DINING ROOM AND THE KITCHEN IS VISUALLY AND PHYSICALLY CUT OFF.

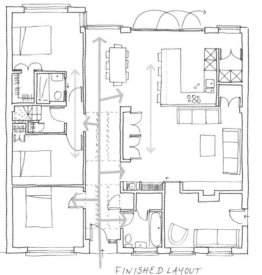

FINISHED LAYOUT

THE FINAL LAYOUT HAS A SIMPLE ENTRANCE HALL WITH A VIEW TO PICTURE A WINDOW OUT TO THE GARDEN. LIGHT FLOODS IN FROM THE RAKED CEILING TO CREATE A FEELING OF HEIGHT. CIRCULATION IS SIMPLIFIED AND THE PRIVATE AND PUBLIC SPACES ARE SEPARATED WHILE MAINTAINING A LIGHT AND AIRY LAYOUT.

Light

Whether you have just moved in or you have lived in the same place for years, we often go onto autopilot when getting on with the hustle of daily life. We rarely step back to observe the spaces we occupy, how the light comes in and the difference it can make to a room. Take some time to consciously work out the areas you gravitate to in your home, and use that to inform your proposed layout ideas.

Design is a balancing act; there are few hard and fast rules. For me, it is about working with what you have, and thinking about your scheme as a whole. You may have the desire for huge amounts of southerly light flooding into to your home, but too much can potentially cause overheating, or you may find yourself constantly pulling down the blinds. In theory, locating rooms such as toilets and utility spaces in the colder north-facing areas, or deep in the dark centre of a house plan, can allow you to open up your layout and design your living spaces outward toward the light. On the flip side, if you lack any direct southerly light, then darker areas can work brilliantly for cosy spaces and snugs.

COAT STORAGE AT THE ENTRANCE IS DISGUISED BEHIND TOUCH-LATCH DOORS WITH THE SKIRTING BOARD CONTINUED AT THE BOTTOM TO MAINTAIN THE VISUAL LINE.

THE VICTORIAN BRICKWORK OF THE ORIGINAL HOUSE IS TIED IN SEAMLESSLY WITH THE NEW WALL CREATING THE KITCHEN AREA. THE LINEAR VIEW IS ENHANCED BY ANGLED ROOF GLAZING WHICH CREATES AN ASYMMETRY AND ALLOWS LIGHT TO FLOOD DOWN.

THE SKYLIGHT IS FRAMELESS, WITH THE WALLS GOING STRAIGHT UP TO MEET THE GLASS. THE LIGHT CAST DOWN FROM THE GLAZING IS SMOOTH, WITH NO WALLS OR STEPS TO CREATE SHADOWS. THE LIGHT ZONES THE SEATING AREA AND LIGHTS THE BREAKFAST BAR TOO.

Let there be light: the roof

If you are extending your home, then adding a new element to the existing building provides a great opportunity to bring light into your space, give real architectural drama and express your style. There are over 30 different varieties of roofs, hipped or valley, mansard or butterfly, single pitch or Dutch gabled. Thankfully they can all be grouped into two basic categories – flat or sloped.

I am not going to describe every roof type in detail, as I cannot imagine it would aid your design process and flow. The aim is not to give you an encyclopaedic knowledge of roof types (who would want to read that?). Instead, I am going to break down and simplify the character of flat and sloped roofs in a more abstract way. This will allow you to picture the impact of your extension and how the roof is not only a great opportunity to bring in light, height and drama, but is also a key component to express your unique architectural style. Having this knowledge will enable you to avoid the common, costly mistake of adding a couple of small, off-the-shelf rooflights to add light to a gloomy extension that is almost fully built.

A SINGLE PITCHED SLOPED ROOF can add height to a space. Following the same slope internally gives you a pitched or raked ceiling inside and is a wonderful and simple way to join two built elements together, opening up opportunities for glazing and lighting. However, if your existing home is already quite long and the ceiling's fairly low, then increasing the space with an extension will not enhance it.

A so-called **FLAT ROOF** is actually very slightly sloped to allow rainwater to run off, but 'very slightly sloped' isn't quite as catchy a title as simply 'flat'. This type of roof is often feared given its cold, leaky reputation of old. But building regulations now mean that any flat roof construction must be thickly insulated and, more crucially, ventilated to ensure a lovely warm roof. Flat roofs, whether or not they have a parapet, can end up being quite high due to the depth required for well-ventilated insulation to meet building standards. It is therefore important to consider the impact on any neighbours when deciding on the roof type. If you would like to include elements such as sedum, grass or wildflower planting on a flat roof, ensure you speak to your engineer as this extra weight will need to be considered in the calculations. You can buy modules to hold a green roof and this is a fantastic and inexpensive way to retrofit the system, providing the roof structure is adequate.

As detailed in the previous chapter, a single-storey extension will rarely provide matching ceiling heights between old and new and glazing can provide a great way to join the two elements.

But how and where can you get the warmth of southerly, westerly or easterly light into your home if your property is north-facing? One option is to look up.

You can choose to glaze in a vast array of different ways. From high-tech to low, exposed rafters to neat frameless glazing, this way of bringing natural light deep into your plan can set the tone of the architectural design. Where extending is not an option, opening up an existing flat ceiling to expose the underside slope of your roof is an effective way of getting direct light, projections or reflections of sunshine into your space. Raking the ceiling above a staircase and introducing glazing can totally transform the space below. If your existing roof structure is structurally sound, then you can glaze directly on top of the existing rafters to give real drama to the stairwell. Off-the-shelf skylights can be a great solution when used thoughtfully. Rather than the ubiquitous side-by-

A BUTTERFLY ROOF CONSISTS OF TWO ANGLED SECTIONS OPPOSITE EACH OTHER LIKE THE WINGS OF A BUTTERFLY. HERE, THE WINGS ARE GLAZED, AND FROM INSIDE THE ROOM THE ROOF OVER THE DINING AREA APPEARS TO BE SUSPENDED.

side small rooflights that you often see, take some time to look at the manufacturer's list of standard sizes with your builder, architect or designer; you will be surprised at the beautiful proportions and large sizes of skylights you can get hold of easily. Working out the best size for your space becomes part of the design process, whether it is a long and thin panel that creates a slice of light, or a large square opening up to the sky, the more unusual off-the-shelf rooflights sizes can look like expensive, bespoke glazing.

By working with your home's unique aspect, you can introduce areas of glazing to the direction of sun that best suit your layout. Big or small, these new windows and skylights will connect you with nature and the dramatic changes through the day and season to season, with natural light becoming an integral part of your design. Bringing in pools of sunlight will not only break up a deep, dark plan but light can be used to define different zones within your floor plan and will help bring your home to life.

Often, just like the ubiquitous box extension itself, no thought is given to where rooflights are installed and are usually popped in, equally spaced, no matter what room is below. Natural light is a brilliant way to zone areas without the need for physical partitioning. Think about what you are lighting below and also how you will see your different glazed elements. Although a large flat skylight above a dining table is lovely in theory, it can

EVEN THOUGH LIGHT IS COMING FROM BOTH THE SIDE AND FROM ABOVE, THE SITTING AND DINING AREAS SEEM CONTAINED AND INTIMATE.

THE PATH FROM THE GARDEN LEADS UP TO THE SLOT WINDOW, MAKING FOR AN ATTRACTIVE VIEW ALL YEAR ROUND.

A SIMPLE SKYLIGHT ABOVE A
FLOOR-TO-CEILING PICTURE
WINDOW CREATES AN UP-
AND-OVER PANORAMIC
VIEW WITHOUT THE COST
OF FRAMELESS GLAZING.
DAY OR NIGHT, SUNSHINE
OR STARS, THE VIEW FROM
THE BED IS UNINTERRUPTED.

often be very bright and hot during the daytime, but in the evening it can feel cold and dark without some clever use of artificial lighting to replace the natural light.

Skylights work beautifully when lined up with whatever is below them, such as a window or, a personal favourite of mine, a window seat. Taking care to line up different elements will look elegant and considered. With that in mind,

creating asymmetry in skylights can be really dramatic. Try to line up just one edge for example, in that way you can offset the placement and size of your skylights without losing the line of flow. It is a simple thing to do, but the overall effect gives a bespoke look without breaking the bank.

Where you can't add any additional roof glazing to bring light in from above, an effective way to include a new aspect of sunlight into your space is to create a 90-degree pop-out extension. The beauty of this type of extension is that it works well no matter the scale. Rather than a full-length extension at the back of your property, by cutting it back, your new extension can face and bring in light from a new aspect that your existing configuration doesn't give. Even a narrow 90-degree extension, building out just the width of a glazed door or window, is a superb way to bring in that extra aspect to your space rather than just a flat rear elevation.

A 90-degree extension can give a feeling of a containment that faces the path of the sun. By incorporating a slim column or disappearing corner you can create a real sense of connection with your outdoor space. Another plus point is that, by not extending the full width of your home, you are not using up too much garden space, the extension will be physically smaller yet still give you the space you need and you can avoid any fixed points such as drainage and manholes.

CLERESTORY WINDOW

A clerestory window is one placed high up on a wall, usually close to the junction where the wall meets the ceiling. They are great for getting light into deep, dark plans. I associate them with 1960s and 1970s houses when they were popular. To avoid a clerestory window looking like a bit of a dated throwback, keep the proportions slightly more unusual, such as long and thin, so as not to emulate that classic letterbox shape. I like to rotate a thin window to create a vertical slot section of glazing that brings light in without using up floor area and it is a great way to zone or separate spaces visually using light. Alternatively, a low, floor-level window can work equally well. As if a clerestory window has slipped all the way down the wall, it can bring natural light in without the worry of solar gain and overheating.

A SLOT WINDOW AT FLOOR LEVEL BRINGS LIGHT IN WITHOUT THE WORRY OF OVERLOOKING OR, INDEED, OVERHEATING IF SOUTH-FACING. IT GIVES A CONTEMPORARY FEEL, AND ALLOWS GLAZING AND LIGHT ON A WALL WITHOUT LOSING VALUABLE WALL SPACE ABOVE.

Storage

Our entire home comprises storage in one way or another. From food and clothes to trinkets and keepsakes, the list is exhaustive. Yet storage is rarely built in or thought about during the design process. Most houses have one single place of storage. The dreaded answer of 'it is under the stairs' when hurriedly looking for something vital still gives me the shivers. The under-stair cupboard is often crammed full of coats, plastic bags stuffed with spare plastic bags, the vacuum cleaner and piles of boxes with well-intentioned but peeling labels. They often house the electricity and gas meters, access to a cellar and sometimes a little toilet is squeezed inside. In the majority of original layout Victorian to mid-20th century house types, the under-stairs cupboard is the only decent-sized, easily accessible storage within the home, so no wonder it doesn't work. The most important thing is not just having a huge, deep single-storage cupboard, but practical spaces that provide a place for impractically shaped objects such as sports kits, ironing boards and vacuum cleaners.

I will go into more detail in the next chapter, where we cover the layout and design of Living, Working and Sleeping spaces. But here, I am going to break down the term 'storage' into its many forms.

A STORAGE LOVER'S TALE: WHERE? HOW MUCH? AND WHY IT'S NEVER ENOUGH

In my many years I have only ever been to one house where the lack of storage wasn't an issue. One. The 1970s house had been remodelled and extended, not well exactly – it was still pretty cold, dark and disjointed – but there were two coat cupboards and space for hooks, under-stair storage and even enough kitchen storage that some of the cupboards were unfilled. It wasn't that there were huge cupboards everywhere, it was just that whoever designed and built the house actually considered the homeowner and their routines.

Planning standards demand storage as part of any new-build house or flat, and require 1 m² (11 sq ft) of storage for a single person occupying a one-bedroom space and 1.5 m² (16 sq ft) for two people sharing. It generously goes up to 4 m² (43 sq ft) for a six-bedroomed home occupied by up to eight people. That averages out at 0.5 m² (5 sq ft) of storage per person. I am sure that, like me, as soon as you combine a suitcase, a box of winter jumpers and a family-sized pack of cornflakes you are already bursting out of your government-assigned space allocation. As well as this space standard being woefully inadequate, many house builders put the entire storage space requirement in one single cupboard that usually houses the meters and electrics, pipe runs and stop cocks as well. As a lot of us know with the under-stair cupboard, under eaves or attic space, the success of storage is not about the volume, it is about the accessibility.

MAKE
IT YOURS

BEND AND BREAK THE RULES

Rules are made to be broken right? It would
be an impossible task to create a set of rules
that exactly fit the age or period of your
home, size of your plot or width of your
garden. The three design rules are there
to help you see design from an architect's
point of view, and more specifically how I
approach it. There may be compromises in
your layout, there might be areas that take
an age to resolve, but adjusting the rules to
create your space is part of the process.

Whether new build or a 17th-century
cottage, looking into the existing layout
of your property can help you understand
how, if any, alterations and extensions have
been made. Unpicking this layout will then
account for odd layouts, strange locations
of bathrooms or a horrifying lack of storage.

FADS AND FASHION

Don't get hung up on the materials and final
finishes at the design stage unless you have
a really clear vision of the style of home you
want to create. If the picture in your head
starts to become a hindrance, for example
trying to crowbar in a double height space
or including glazed internal partitions no
matter what, then take a step back and look
at your plan in black and white.

Where your overall vision drives your
design forward, then that is a positive thing
and can be integrated into your design. In
my opinion, if you are true to the intention
of your design, not trying to create a
pastiche or copy your neighbour, when
interior styles come in and out of fashion,
your love for your design will endure. That's
all that really matters.

SCULPTING YOUR SPACE

When you picture someone sculpting clay
on a pottery wheel, it is not a static process.
Every squeeze and nudge creates a shape
or deformity somewhere else in the wet,
spinning mass. That is what you are doing
to your home, every wall that is altered and
layout idea that is tweaked has a knock-on
implication somewhere else, either opening
up a lovely opportunity such as turning
the bottom of a staircase to create new
usable space or separating bedrooms with
wardrobes providing storage and sound
deadening at the same time. Apply and
play around with the three rules of light,
flow and storage to form your space in
three dimensions.

Living + sleeping

Imagine your home as an onion. Not the shape or the smell, but the layers. Like onions, homes have layers. Peel back every layer of your home until you get to the best place of all – your bed. For most of us, it is the place of extreme comfort and rest and something that, like food, we all have in common.

On the face of it, using the simple organization technique of separating the public and private spaces in your home sounds very formal, but in fact it is a fantastic way to integrate flow within your home. The living areas are where you entertain, and the sleeping areas are generally only for the people who live there. If the first view when you come into a home is of your bedroom door, then it will feel a bit exposed. Unless you are incredibly tidy and you want everyone who enters your house to know it, then your bedroom door will be permanently shut in order for you to retain any feel of ownership of the most intimate of space in your home. That is until your bed is hidden under a huge pile of guests coats at a party, and there is always a stray scarf or two left. Always.

In single-level layouts such as flats and bungalows, this physical or visual split is not always easy. I will show you how to create that feeling of privacy and separation by looking at several methods across typical house types but with a focus on single-storey homes, because these tend to be the trickiest homes to create this hierarchy without a staircase to create a split between the living and sleeping floors.

I always like to split the living and the sleeping areas in a home. This is easier in some house types. For example, a typical 1940s semi-detached house was designed with the living, kitchen and dining on the ground floor and the bedrooms and bathroom on the first floor. In a Victorian terrace, while the living spaces and kitchen are generally on the ground floor, the family bathroom – that was not an original feature of most standard houses built in the late 1800s – is often at the rear of the ground floor. Splitting the bedrooms and the bathroom across both two or three floors and across the living space is far from ideal. A typical way around this is to sacrifice one of the bedrooms on the upper floor to accommodate a bathroom. This is a great solution that leaves you with a generous sized bathroom, the downside being you lose a whole bedroom. There are other slightly less conventional ways, of course, such as having a more compact staircase allowing you to install a tiny yet functional family bathroom. More on this later.

Separating living + sleeping

With any house or flat, no matter how vast and sprawling or compact and bijoux it is, one of the first things I seek to organize is the separation between living and sleeping spaces. As I am sure you will agree, our homes do much more than allow us to simply live and sleep within their walls, so if we think about the areas and rooms in terms of the activities that usually take place within them, then we can sort our homes into simple 'public' and 'private' categories. These terms sound rather dry and architectural, but please bear with me, I promise it will make sense. For me, the public spaces in my home are the areas I rush around quickly tidying before guests arrive, and the private spaces are where I shove all the clutter. Maybe you can relate? If we think about the living room, it is definitely a public space in most homes where we bring our guests to sit and chat.

The bedroom is very much a 'sleeping' space and mostly private at night. Mostly. Sometimes, as I touched on previously, where there is very little storage in the entrance to a home, the end of the bed becomes a coat and bag repository. There are also crossover spaces, rooms that are both private and public and accessed off public areas or based in the private areas of the home.

Categorizing the spaces allows you to ascertain how your home and how you live are reflected in each other so that you can see design solutions. You may require a completely private, quiet dedicated home office or a loud breakout play space just off your kitchen.

Once we have identified the public and private areas in the home, we can explore ways to separate, divide, link and join them to create closed, open and broken-plan layouts to suit your lifestyle and needs.

PUBLIC

EASILY ACCESSIBLE AREAS OF THE HOME DESIGNED FOR ENTERTAINING YOU, FAMILY AND GUESTS

Entrance hall
Coat store
WC
Living room
Reception room
Open-plan kitchen and dining area
Open-plan access to garden or
outside space

SEMI-PUBLIC
AREAS THAT ARE OFF
PUBLIC OR LIVING AREAS,
BUT NOT IMMEDIATELY
ACCESSIBLE TO GUESTS

Closed or broken-plan kitchen
Closed or broken-plan dining room
Partly enclosed larder or pantry space
Partly enclosed utility space
Reading nooks or breakout spaces
Playroom areas
Home office area
Guest bedroom
Guest ensuite

SEMI-PRIVATE
CLOSED OFF AREAS OR
ROOMS THAT ARE OFF THE
PRIVATE SLEEPING AREAS
OF THE HOME

Hidden or enclosed larder or pantry
Hidden or enclosed utility room
Family bathroom if accessible or only WC
in the home
Landing, hall or corridor to bedrooms
Guest or spare room
Playroom
Home office

PRIVATE
INDIVIDUAL AREAS THAT
ARE DESIGNED FOR HOME
OWNERS ALONE TO SLEEP
AND DRESS, WORK OR RELAX

Bedrooms
Ensuite bath or shower rooms to
bedrooms
Walk-in wardrobes
Bedroom sitting areas
Bedroom terrace or garden access
Dedicated home office

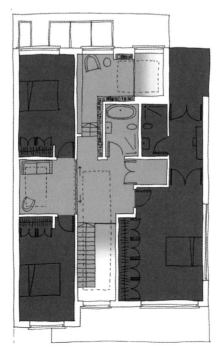

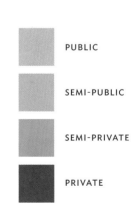

PUBLIC

SEMI-PUBLIC

SEMI-PRIVATE

PRIVATE

Physical + visual divides

TYPICAL LIVING ROOM LAYOUTS

CIRCULATION OFTEN
CROSSES DIAGONALLY
THROUGH ROOMS

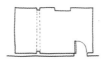

REMOVING A DIVIDING
WALL CAN CREATE
A LONG THIN ROOM

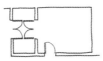

DOUBLE DOORS OPENING
OPPOSITE A FEATURE
CAN CREATE A GOOD
SNUG ROOM

BRING DOORS CLOSER
TOGETHER TO MAXIMISE
USABLE SPACE.
MULTIFUNCTIONAL
SPACE CAN REDUCE THE
LENGTH TO GIVE FLOW
AND FUNCTION

TYPICAL LAYOUT OF ADJACENT ROOMS

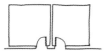

DOORS OFF A CORRIDOR
ACCESSING INDIVIDUAL
ROOMS

OFFSETTING THE
TWO DOORS ALLOWS
EACH DOOR TO FEEL
MORE PRIVATE

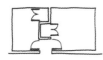

THE SPACE BETWEEN
THE ROOMS CAN BE
STAGGERED TO GIVE
STORAGE TO EACH ROOM

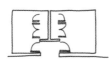

INCREASING THE DEPTH
OF THE STORAGE ALLOWS
FULL WIDTH CUPBOARDS
TO EACH ROOM

Physically dividing off a room doesn't just mean adding a door, although historically it is the most common way to do it. Closing the door to every room in the house leads to dark and confusing hallways and no clear distinction between public and private spaces. How many times have you asked where the loo is, only to be given a complex set of directions? Home design ultimately seeks to simplify and improve your life through the clarity of design, light and seamless functionality. Like nearly everything in life, dividing your space is a sliding scale: some activities need to be firmly behind a closed door and others can merge public and private.

Visual separation can be created using anything from partial walls, large open doors, curtains or even lighting. Layering, as we looked at in Cracking common design problems (see page 50), brings depth and interest and allows you to animate your circulation route and create focal points within your layout, elevating the space from what could easily become a corridor to a piece of architecture.

There is an infinite number of ways to configure the heart of the home. We have already touched on the concepts of open-, broken- and closed-plan layouts, and how the intensity of the connections between the spaces can drastically alter the drama and practicality of a home.

Even in the most open of open-plan spaces, I always like to incorporate some sort of zoning. Whether that is a partial wall, an open bookshelf or partial screening, the reality of living in a fully open-plan space is often underestimated.

Let's look at different ways we can both physically and visually divide spaces within the home as a whole, and also activities within rooms. Like any design standard, these elements will be shaped and adapted to work within your home whether it is an elegant Georgian town house or a 1980s bungalow in need of full restoration.

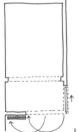

A DISAPPEARING CORNER OPENS UP TWO ROOMS. PANEL DOORS FOLD BACK AND SIT AGAINST ONE WALL SECTION AND A LARGE, PERPENDICULAR PANEL SLIDES BACK TO LINK THE TWO SPACES.

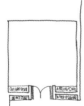

THE OPEN LEAVES OF A DOUBLE DOOR SIT BACK AGAINST THE WALL, CONTAINED WITHIN A THICKENED WALL WITH STORAGE AND BOOKSHELVES. USE THIS METHOD TO HIDE STRUCTURE OR PIPES.

AN OVERSIZED OPENING VISUALLY CONNECTS A GAMES, TV OR OFFICE NOOK OFF A MAIN SPACE. A SECTION OF WALL FROM AN OFFSET OPENING HIDES A SOFA AND CHAIR.

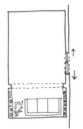

LENGTHENING A ROOM MAY LEAVE STUB WALLS TO TAKE THE STEEL BEAM ABOVE. DISGUISE THIS WITH A BESPOKE SEATING AREA, INFILL THE EXTENDED WALLS WITH SHELVING.

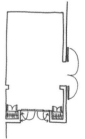

TO OPEN UP A ROOM WITHOUT CREATING A CROSS THROUGH ROUTE THAT DISRUPTS THE SPACE LOCATE THE DOORS FAIRLY CLOSE TO EACH OTHER. THIS SIMPLIFIES THE CIRCULATION.

Home working

Working from home is a fixture in most of our lives. Whether you are full-time, part-time or somewhere in between, being able to integrate your home into your working life is simultaneously a benefit and a burden. On the face of it, finding a home office space can be as easy as clearing a space on the dining table or getting comfy on the sofa and working on your knee. For the vast majority of us, the novelty of this has started to wear rather thin. The disruption of having to clear away books, laptops and files before you can lay the table or sit down for a restful evening can take its toll. Although on paper it seems like a minor ordeal, the reality of having to hot desk with your child or cat can be somewhat challenging.

I set up my own architectural practice over ten years ago and started working from my bedroom in a shared flat. I didn't want to see my work, files and computer when lying in bed so I utilized an old 1920s radiogram that was my grandfather's as my office. This allowed me to close it in the evenings – when it was tidy enough to be physically able to squish everything in. I still have the radiogram in my bedroom and it has been upgraded to my makeup table. The nightly battle to close it and the fight against my expanding clutter are ongoing.

In the home, the doubling up of function where space is at a premium is a complex design problem to solve. Having started my architectural practice within the comfort (or lack of it) and beauty of a vintage radiogram, I have never really liked the idea of going back to a conventional, formal desk and high-backed office chair, especially if the space will be shared with another function like a dining room, guest bedroom or even the kitchen. My current workspace is a 1960s Danish writing desk that I bought for £90 ($104) a few years ago and despite the fact that I can't open the drawers when I am sitting at it, it looks great. Don't tell anyone, but sometimes I choose to compromise practicality over looks.

Like most elements in our daily lives, the requirements for your home office can vary greatly. It is important that any designed space reflects the complexity of being able to perform your tasks with ease, in a space that provides inspiration and comfort. A spare bedroom can be a brilliant and practical home office, but having a dedicated space that does not need to perform any other function is a rare luxury. Whether you are regularly conducting lengthy online meetings and phone calls, or you simply need a space to organize household bills, the structure of your home office has to fit within the overall layout, changing and adapting where necessary. In a way, the demands of a home office are similar to those of a playroom, crafting

THE 100-YEAR-OLD INHERITED RADIOGRAM, THAT WAS MY FIRST SELF-CONTAINED WORKSPACE IS SEEING OUT ITS LATER LIFE AS A DRESSING TABLE AND STORE FOR MY MAKE-UP.

A SMALL, NARROW OFFICE SPACE NEXT TO THE LIVING SPACE CAN BE CLOSED OFF WITH BIFOLD SLIDING DOORS ON ONE OR BOTH SIDES, ALLOWING ONLINE MEETINGS TO BE CARRIED OUT WITHOUT DISRUPTION.

A LARGER OFFICE AT THE BACK OF THE HOUSE COULD CLOSE OFF THE GARDEN. TO MAINTAIN THE VIEW THROUGH THE HOUSE, ALIGN THE SLIDING PANEL DOOR TO THE OFFICE WITH THE ENTRANCE DOOR, ENTRANCE HALL, AND THE GLAZED GARDEN DOORS.

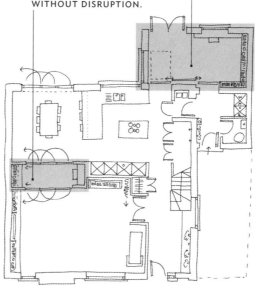

AN INFREQUENTLY USED DESK CAN BE CONTAINED IN A CUPBOARD. FOLD-BACK OR PIVOT SLIDING DOORS THAT HIDE IN A POCKET ARE IDEAL.

IF SPACE IS AT A PREMIUM, CONTINUE THE ROOM DÉCOR INTO THE DESK SPACE TO INTEGRATE IT. THINK ABOUT HOW IT LOOKS WHEN NOT IN USE.

space or art studio, and should be equally as fun and inspirational yet practical.

TIME How much time do you expect to spend in your home office overall? If you are spending a full working day in a space carved out in a cubby hole with your office storage stashed away elsewhere, then it will never feel comfortable or easy to concentrate in.

SPACE What area do you need to work in? What equipment is needed? Do you need a contained area or an inspiring background for online meetings?

VIEWS What is more important to you, a window toward the entrance of your home for easy acceptance of deliveries, visitors or clients, or an inspiring view to an open space, garden or terrace? Where that isn't possible, create a focus within your workspace using a gallery wall, mirrors or plants and decoration.

Thinking through and plotting out the use of your office will help you zone the workspace itself as well as how it sits in your home. If you regularly host visitors, whether in a studio or treatment space, create access in and out, and ensure coat storage and the toilet don't directly impede on your home. Think about your needs, from loo breaks to kitchen visits. Sadly, there are few or no watercooler moments in the home office, but having a relaxing space within your kitchen or living area can feel like a small retreat from work and the stresses of running the home.

Where floor area is limited, you may be able to squeeze in a small desk space under the stairs or in a corridor. Lining up doors or removing unnecessary ones can free up wall space that can be used as a work zone. Similarly, if you have a staircase, creating a winder by turning the bottom or top few steps can open up enough space for an office nook. I will go into detail about finding and creating additional floor area in Maximizing your space (page 148).

Where a more conventionally sized office room is needed, but a connection with the rest of the home is desired, creating a glazed wall will give privacy and reduce noise, yet maintain light and views to the rest of the home. A floor-to-ceiling curtain within a space or in front of a glazed wall can give quick, super low-tech and cost-effective visual separation. Different fabrics give distinct effects, be it diffusing the light, blocking it out altogether, or simply bring pattern and style to your workspace. Alternatively, think about separating the space without using a standard door configuration. Wide sliding panels, interior bifold doors, double doors, sliding pocket doors or even a folding screen can seamlessly open up or close off a space when needed.

A home-working area can be zoned as part of an open-plan living space by using a section of floor-to-ceiling storage. With the addition of fold-back pocket doors, you can open up a large section of desk space, complete with file storage, shelving and even printer space without the need to tidy everything away when not in use – simply close the doors to hide it.

Another simple solution where space is tight is a fold-down table. Choose one with a deep frame and the face of the frame becomes the desk and the depth of the frame can be used for storage. This also works brilliantly for play, craft or homework spaces too. Wireless or Bluetooth printers and scanners can be hidden away in a cupboard if rarely used, or within conveniently placed storage if needed regularly. Where specialist cabling such as Cat 6 or above is required, or you anticipate a large number of sockets, plan these into your design and your brief to ensure you aren't installing wiring retrospectively or having to deal with endless extension cables.

A garden office is a brilliant alternative to a home office if you have the space and budget. Think about the views in and out, outdoor lighting and the route back to the house in the winter.

A FOLDING TIMBER SCREEN IS A SIMPLE WAY TO DIVIDE A SPACE. CONNECTING ONE EDGE TO THE WALL MAKES IT EASY TO OPEN AND CLOSE WITHOUT THE RISK OF IT TOPPLING OVER.

Working + playing

Successful living spaces are difficult to design, especially where there are several generations in the home. You must not only think about how you live now, but how you may see yourself using the space next month, next year and maybe some five years on. Trying to find ways to separate the more grown-up living spaces from the piles of toys and games that often accumulate in the corner is a tricky one. 'Toy creep' is a common issue in homes, especially with small children. Sometimes, where there is space, dedicated playrooms can be a great addition. However, as we have seen all the way through this book, the placement of a playroom often poses more problems than it solves.

Younger children nearly always want to be close to their parents, grandparents or caregivers. All children are different, but generally there are times in their lives when a shut-away space far away from the heart of the home will not work for either of you. It is about finding balance. You do not want to end up designing a space that works brilliantly for a child in their infancy, when they are generally happy to sit or lie in one place for hours, but then starts to fail when they want to bring toys, books and stuffed animals in to show you.

For me, designing a play space is very similar to designing a home office. If you think about it, the fundamental elements you need are the same: storage, surface, space and separation. The main difference comes in the amount of each you need. For a child, you will need plenty of easily accessible, shallow storage so that their toys and games are easy to find, and, more importantly, easy to put away. They may need a surface for painting or Lego, but maybe if they are less mobile, then a desk space may not be needed. They probably need more space than a basic home office set up, but the ability to separate

A DIVIDING WALL HIDES THE STRUCTURE TO GIVE A FEELING OF AN OPEN-PLAN LIVING, KITCHEN AND DINING AREA YET IT ONLY GIVES A LITTLE VISUAL SEPARATION. STORAGE AS DISPLAY CREATES A FOCUS TO THE ROOM, AND THE CONTINUITY OF THE BIRCH PLYWOOD GIVES THE EFFECT OF BESPOKE JOINERY.

or shut off a working space is often crucial where a bit of quiet is needed. In terms of future-proofing, if you can design a space that works equally well for play, work or even just sitting down with a coffee and a book then, by its very design, it will stand the test of time.

We will look at how these spaces can fit into home layouts in the next chapter, but for now let's look at some ways in which, by using storage, we can create spaces to play, work and sometimes both at the same time.

If we look at cupboards as more than just a handy static storage vessel, then we can work with the component parts to zone and form space. Open shelving and seating work well as a quiet space, with the option for doors or walls to separate off the space if needed. Thinking about the cupboard doors in a different way, as more than just things to be opened or closed, we can see how they can be used to separate and create areas, forming walls themselves, or disappear into a concealed pocket space.

The inside face of a child's storage doors can provide a canvas, pin board or even a Lego base plate. Wide double doors can open up and sit back again the wall so they can be drawn on and used as part of their play. When open they could form a small internal area, creating a den-like space. The bigger these spaces become the more they are allowed to become small, self-contained areas that lend themselves brilliantly to office space or, when expanded further, even a cinema room.

We will delve into the details and look at examples of how to lay out these spaces with respect to the rest of the living spaces, your kitchen, dining, living and play areas, as well as looking at bedrooms and bathrooms in the next chapter.

CLOSED OFFICE
V. OPEN OFFICE

Working from home is a concept that divides us. Some love it, some hate it. But for those who don't enjoy it but must endure it in some form, I wonder whether not having a dedicated space might be the root of the problem. Locking yourself into a spare bedroom, being crammed into a glorified cupboard or having to share your desk space with the rest of the family is pretty uninspiring when you have a hard day of work ahead.

Not many homes can dedicate a whole room or zone to working, and for most, carving out an office space within your existing layout, or designing in a dedicated working space, must still include a great deal of flexibility. Being able to fully close off an office is a necessity for some lines of work, whether that is for concentration, quiet or even if you see clients or customers in your home. But sacrificing a bedroom or snug to be able to do this is a big ask in most homes. Being able to hide away your office storage is the most obvious place to start, but how to do this, is the question.

It is important to have an inspiring view or visual focus when sitting at your desk in order to maintain motivation, plus you need easy access to the loo and kitchen. Where an office space is located by a window, losing that window when the office is closed off is not ideal. Using the original three design principles of **FLOW**, **LIGHT** and **STORAGE** means you can zone the space and ensure the living element of the layout maintains the view out. By keeping a clear line of flow and positioning the storage so that it is offset from that line you will allow light in and retain the views out. Then, even if your office is used as a dedicated workspace for the majority of the week, it can become part of the home when free. Likewise, where home working is only sporadic or temporary, the flexibility of the space is more important. These plans illustrating various configurations all show solid walls for simplicity. Use glazed walls and doors, flush, hidden doors or materials, texture and colour to either express or disguise these home offices.

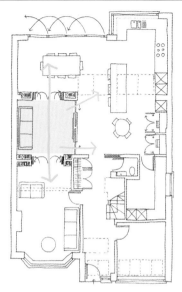

A CINEMA ROOM MAKES AN IDEAL TEMPORARY OFFICE SPACE. IT CAN BE CLOSED OR OPENED UP TO THE MAIN SPACE. THE DIVIDING WALLS HIDE STRUCTURE AND CREATE DISPLAY AND STORAGE AREAS.

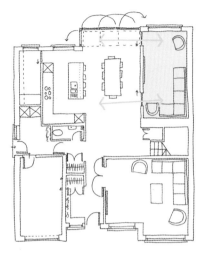

ALIGN THE SLIDING DOORS OF A SNUG, PLAYROOM OR OFFICE WITH OVERHEAD GLAZING AND EXTERNAL CORNER BIFOLD DOORS TO GIVE AN ELEGANT LINE. THE OPEN DOORS CREATE A CIRCULAR CIRCULATION SO THE SPACE LOOKS COMPLETE.

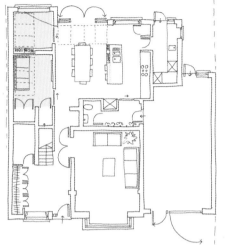

A LONG, THIN PLAN WITH FEW WINDOWS TO THE REAR MEANS THIS OFFICE TAKES UP AN ENTIRE WINDOW. A SLIDING WALL SEPARATES IT WHEN REQUIRED. AS THE ROOM BEHIND HAS NO DIRECT LIGHT, IT IS AN IDEAL CINEMA OR GAMING ROOM.

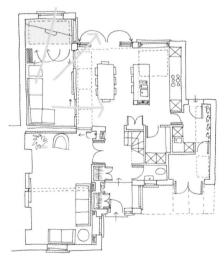

ANOTHER WAY TO RESOLVE A LONG, THIN LIVING SPACE WITH AN OFFICE ATTACHED IS TO ALLOW THE WHOLE DIVIDING WALL TO DISAPPEAR. THE SLIDING POCKET DOORS TO THE CENTRAL TV WALL OPEN UP THE SNUG WHEN SEPARATED FROM THE OFFICE.

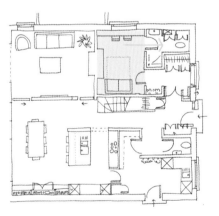

A CLOSED OFF, PERMANENT OFFICE ROOM IS LOCATED NEAR A WC AND SHOWER ROOM ON THE GROUND FLOOR. THIS IS IDEAL IF THE ROOM IS TO DOUBLE UP AS A SPARE BEDROOM, ESPECIALLY WHEN USED BY GUESTS WITH LIMITED MOBILITY.

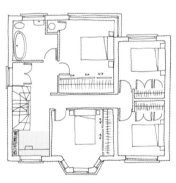

AN OFFICE NOOK CREATED FROM THE SPACE GAINED BY MAKING THE STAIRCASE MORE SPACE EFFICIENT BENEFITS FROM ELEVATED VIEWS OUT. IT IS SEPARATED FROM THE HEART OF THE HOME BUT HAS EASY ACCESS TO IT.

Zoning spaces

Simplicity is key to design. As there are so many factors to consider when working out how to connect the kitchen, dining and living spaces, this part of the design is tricky to perfect. For most individuals and families, it is the heart of the home and getting it right is crucial. Families grow and change, merge and divide, and if we choose, or have to, stay in our homes for the long term then the heart of the home must adapt to our changing personal circumstances and needs, accessibility and age.

I have been given a lot of plans over the years, some that have been accepted all the way through the planning process, and nine times out of ten the kitchen and dining space has been left as a large open space with no thought or indication as to how to zone or divide the space. In lieu of a detailed kitchen and dining layout, there will just be a large blank space stating 'KITCHEN DINER' or better yet, an even larger area brazenly entitled 'FAMILY ROOM' that I assume includes the addition of a bit of living space too. Although kitchen design isn't rocket science, it is a highly time-consuming process as you must think about how you use the space every morning, noon and night, on special occasions and also with thoughts to future needs too.

Zoning spaces, especially in more open-plan designs can be done with lighting, either artificial or natural, changes in floor levels or by creating space where no circulation cuts through. Before we look at how and where to connect the kitchen, dining and living spaces, let's first get a deep understanding of the layout of the kitchen, the powerhouse of the home.

IN THIS LIVING SPACE AN L-SHAPED COUCH IS POSITIONED SO THAT THE ORIGINAL FIREPLACE, NOW CLAD IN BIRCH PLYWOOD WITH AN INSET TELEVISION AND GUITAR DISPLAY AND STORAGE, IS THE FOCUS. IT IS OFF THE CIRCULATION ROUTE AND THE FLOOR AREA IS ZONED TO GIVE A FEELING OF COMFORT. THE CONTINUITY OF MATERIALS ON THE FLOOR AND WALLS THROUGHOUT THE GROUND FLOOR CREATES FLOW, WHILE THE ZONING IS DEFINED BY THE CIRCULATION. THE PINK, LOW-LEVEL DIVIDING WALL FURTHER EMPHASIZES THE COSINESS.

Types of kitchen

Despite the seemingly endless variety of layouts, there is a limited number of kitchen layout types. We aren't going to look at styles such as Shaker or ultra-minimal, as this doesn't address the real backbone of the kitchen layout. Once we have the backbone or skeleton of the design, the kitchen will stand the test of time no matter what style you want to achieve or indeed change to over the years.

KITCHEN ISLAND OR PENINSULA

I like to lump these together as the island is essentially just separated from the main run. The two types work in a similar way in terms of layout.

GALLEY KITCHEN

Galley kitchens are my favourite, yet they are the kind of kitchens that strike fear into the heart of most homeowners, mainly because I think generally it sounds like a really small galley of a boat or a ship. I find they have a lot of potential in terms of design, and you can see the similarity between an island-type kitchen and a galley as they are closely related.

THE C-SHAPE

A flattened, squat C-shaped kitchen can work very well in the layouts of many flats or houses, from a typical Victorian villa all the way up to a 1940s house where the ground floor layout has a dining room, often with a chimney breast in the room opposite a narrow galley kitchen. The kitchen is often visible from the entrance hall and, while extending out to the side is not possible, there is not enough width within the old kitchen set up to install a new kitchen layout comfortably without seeing the kitchen when you walk through the front door. Flipping the kitchen to put it in the old dining room works well in the majority of cases, with the final tweaks to any existing chimney breast being the main sticking point. Where the chimney breast ends up central to the new kitchen layout it can be a great place to install the hob, venting out either through the existing chimney stack or in flat ducting within the wall to the outside. The chimney breast can be taken out altogether, giving more floor area in the proposed kitchen, and this allows for the wall dividing off the kitchen to be offset from the line of symmetry of the chimney breast.

Long and thin C-shaped kitchens can stretch and fill a similarly long and thin room, turning at the bottom to create the opportunity for a small breakfast bar or the placement of a kitchen window. This is a similar layout to that of the peninsula kitchen, but with no exposed run which as a result minimizes the seating possibilities.

THE KITCHEN AS A ROOM IN THE HOME

I think that 'the kitchen as a room in the home' demands its own category. More than an elaborate kitchen diner, this is a great way to incorporate a working kitchen into a smaller house or flat where the kitchen is a prominent element and it will become a design feature on its own merits. It works well where the kitchen is located in a room where there are features such as panelling, elaborate coving and picture rails. The kitchen is essentially designed as an enlarged piece of furniture that complements the proportions and style of the room.

Although this category isn't so much a layout type as a lifestyle choice, if this is something that you are looking to achieve in your home then getting the bones right is key, no matter what the style, hence my adding it as a separate category.

For this style, there are certain types of kitchen layouts that lend themselves to certain house eras. For example, a typical Victorian terrace works really well with a C-shaped kitchen within the darker middle room, allowing the dining and sitting space to open up to the back of the house, typically toward the garden or outdoor space.

SINGLE-WALL TYPE

The single-wall kitchen is simplicity itself. It reminds me of an old country kitchen, where the large, wooden dining table, passed down from generation to generation, sits silently as the centrepiece to family life as it unfolds around it. Used well, the single wall type can give a really contemporary look and it is not cheating if the main bulk of storage is hidden behind floor-to-ceiling doors opposite it.

This simple, sleek kitchen style is not always the most practical in terms of use, mainly because the storage is often up high to make the most of the space, but it looks great in terms of simplicity.

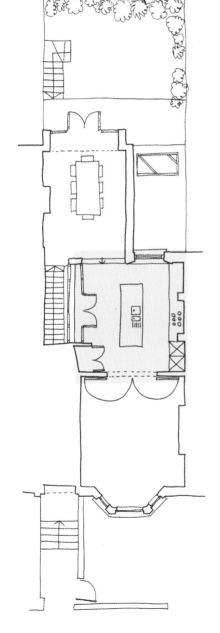

THE L-SHAPE

Where there is not the depth for a full C-shaped kitchen, an L-shape works brilliantly. It provides an elegant right angle to frame an oversized, square kitchen island, or even seating and works wonders when there isn't quite enough depth for a C-shape.

L-shaped kitchens work well in small spaces, with the triangle of preparation – the idea that a kitchen's three main work areas of the sink, refrigerator and stove should form a triangle – pretty much integral to the layout. It ensures there is no footfall through this area.

STORAGE AS DISPLAY. WHETHER OPENED OR CLOSED, THIS SHALLOW WALL-TO-WALL SHELVING PROVIDES HUGE AMOUNTS OF PRACTICAL, ACCESSIBLE STORAGE. THE CONTENTS ARE THE STYLE DRIVER AND FOCUS OF THE KITCHEN AND, INDEED, THE ENTIRE BROKEN-PLAN LAYOUT.

How to design your kitchen

We can now bring together everything you have learned from the first section of this book, and concentrate on the heart of the home. This is usually where I start with any design as it tends to be the main focus.

First, refresh your brief. To ensure you are thinking about the bigger picture and not getting bogged down in the minutiae of where your dishwasher and fridge should go, hold your home dream scenario in your mind, whether that is a bustling kitchen island or a quiet sunny window seat. This is important throughout the design process.

By now, you will have marked the north point on your floor plan and will understand how the path of the sun moves around and lights your home. You will have drawn on the existing circulation routes and identified where the current layout falls apart.

Turning the plan in the direction that you walk through means you can almost 'see' how the existing layout is formed in front of you. Plus you can work out if a direct route or view through the space is possible. As noted previously, a view through doesn't always need to lead out to an outdoor space or garden, it can be a vista through your home, leading you from the entrance to your initial most desirable space.

Creating a straight sightline from the entrance is the first and most crucial step. It becomes the spine of circulation that the layout is shaped on. Sometimes this isn't possible, it may be slightly cranked or offset, but we will cover such eventualities shortly.

WORKING WITH THE ORIGINAL FEATURES OF A HOME OR ROOM IS KEY WHEN INTEGRATING A KITCHEN INTO A ROOM THAT WAS NOT DESIGNED TO BE ONE. THIS ORIGINAL DOORWAY HAS BEEN PARTIALLY BLOCKED UP, BUT THE DEEP VOID IS USED FOR GLASS STORAGE AND DISPLAY.

The sightline

The initial sightline is everything. It outlines the area and space you have to work with and largely determines the initial zoning of the design. If you want a specific type of kitchen, such as an island or C-shaped kitchen, then it is critical that you determine the minimal dimensions at this stage. In the vast majority of designs, I try to avoid having circulation or a view to cut through the triangle of preparation (see page 128) as this is where the action happens. For example, if the triangle of preparation is also the main access to a garden or terrace, you will be constantly tripping over the chef; or, if you have a line of sight straight through it, you will always be looking at the kitchen sink. It will also make the kitchen area feel more spacious, even if the actual dimensions are on the tight side. There are always exceptions, and design rules are there to be bent and broken, so we will look at how to approach variations on this theme in the coming chapters.

Rooms are rarely square, plumb and true. When renovating or remodelling old properties, the lack of any right angle or straight wall can become a bit of a running joke. When you want to install a kitchen into a room that was never intended to become a modern-day kitchen you can run into a number of design conundrums. You often have to contend with windowsills that are much lower or higher than the finished kitchen worktop level of 900 mm (35.4 in.) from floor level. Structures like chimney breasts or cupboards built into the walls, called 'presses' in Scotland and Ireland, are among the things that your layout may have to incorporate. Rather than working against these features, by planning around them, they can become highly advantageous to your design.

THE LINE OF SIGHT IS KEY TO IMPOSE SIMPLICITY ON AN AWKWARDLY SHAPED PLAN. THE SIGHTLINE IMMEDIATELY SHOWS HOW THE SPACES AND ZONES COME TOGETHER, WITH NO FEELING THAT GUESTS DON'T KNOW WHERE TO GO. THE FLOW POINTS TO THE HEART OF THE HOME.

The inventor of the triangle of preparation

Many will have heard of the phrase 'triangle of preparation' and, indeed, the peddle waste bin. But what you might not know is that they were invented by the same person. Until I started writing this book, neither did I. Lillian Moller Gilbreth (1878–1972) was born in Oakland, California, US, and was a psychologist, industrial engineer and one of the first women ever to earn a Ph.D. Her pioneering work into the ergonomic use of the home resulted in her invention of the triangle of preparation, which remains the most accepted and commonly used design standard today.

After carrying out further research, I discovered that she took a positive stance toward eugenics. I want to express my abject abhorrence and rejection of her political, ethical and racist views. Yet, as the achievements of female scientists, architects, and engineers are finally being recognized on an equal footing to their male counterparts, I feel it would be remiss of me not to mention her academic work and its enduring impact.

I want to pose a fresh take on kitchens here, rather than rehashing generic material on the layout and function of these rooms.

THE TRIANGLE OF PREPARATION BETWEEN THE FRIDGE, FREEZER AND HOB IS UNINTERRUPTED BY THE CIRCULATION ROUTE THROUGH THE LAYOUT.

EVEN IN A SMALLER
KITCHEN LAYOUT, THE
TRIANGLE OF PREPARATION
IS CONTAINED BEHIND THE
ISLAND, SEPARATING IT
FROM THE ENTERTAINMENT
AND DINING SPACE.

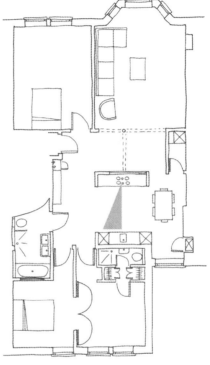

IN AN OPEN OR BROKEN
PLAN LAYOUT, KEEP
THE TRIANGLE OF
PREPARATION NEAT
AND COMPACT. THEN,
NO MATTER THE SIZE OF
THE KITCHEN OR SPACES
SURROUNDING, THE
WORKING SPACE WILL
BE EFFICIENT AND FEEL
CONTAINED.

Dimensions in kitchens

In stark contrast to the very limited number of kitchen types, there are infinite ways to lay out the rest of the rooms and spaces around it. It is like a Rubik's cube of possibilities. But when, after many sketches and design attempts, your kitchen layout slots into place in your design, the heart of the home starts to come together. So let's look in depth at how to plan a kitchen that suits you and your surroundings, as well as your lifestyle and your dreams.

I always use the line of flow established in the previous chapters as the outline for the layout of a kitchen. This allows us to keep the view

through, and the floor space and circulation route completely uninterrupted, unless you choose to break it up, articulating your style and preference.

This is the design method that I have established over the years to explore ways of setting out the different kitchen types. Bear in mind that houses and flats are never identical, so once you have digested this next section, we will look at how to bend and flex these rules to fit your needs while always ensuring the basis of good design.

The practical dimensions needed for most kitchen layouts are very

similar. Using the standard width of kitchen units and worktops, we know that our island will be 900 mm (35.4 in.) wide and the unit opposite will be 600 mm (23.6 in.) wide. Ideally, we must retain a distance of 1200 mm (47.2 in.) between the face of the island or peninsula and the units facing it. That gives the internal width of 2,700 mm (106.2 in.) which is required to comfortably fit these kitchen types within the space. If you are a little short of space, then the island can be reduced down to 600 mm (23.6 in.), with the potential for a staggered breakfast bar arrangement to help minimize the dimensions. Plus the distance between the two opposite unit runs can be squeezed down to a minimum of 1100 mm (43.3 in.). The reason for this critical dimension is that it allows you to freely walk behind someone else and open the oven door safely too. Safety is my middle name. Well, one of them. So if you are struggling for width and dream of having a kitchen island, you can get away with a minimal internal width of 2,300 mm (90.5 in.). A hundred millimetres here, 50 millimetres there, it all adds up when you are working in more restricted houses or flats. Likewise, you can expand these dimensions too, in order to comfortably make the layout fit your space.

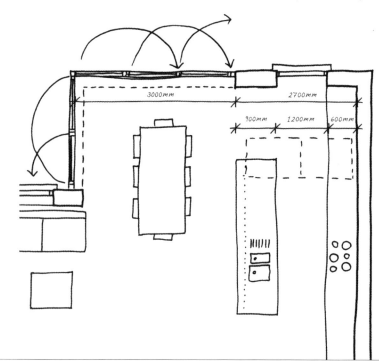

One thing I always ensure is that the kitchen sink cannot be seen from the main the circulation route. This is so unbelievably common, I can't quite fathom it. With the best will in the world, without employing dedicated full-time kitchen staff, or a strictly enforced dishwasher-filling code of conduct, then the kitchen sink is the last thing I want to see as I walk in through my front door. However, I have alluded to my untidy nature before, so I know that has a large influence on my kitchen sink bugbear.

When you follow these minimum dimensions, it means that you don't have an island poking out into your line of flow and view when you walk in through the front door. Although it is sometimes beneficial to line it up with the edge of the island or peninsula, so you can see bar stools for example, giving a visual clue to guests of where to go. It also means that the style and type of bar stool can be a considered choice and changed up when you change the style of the space.

Dining spaces should always be a minimum width of 3000 mm (118 in.), that is 1000 mm (39.3 in.) for the table and 1000 mm (39.3 in.) either side for access when you have a guest sitting there, without the need for them to pull the chair in.

These all seem rather rigid dimensions and widths, but what happens when you don't have these neat comfortable spaces in your home? As with everything in architecture and interiors, the guidelines are just that, they are designed to be flexible, to mould your space and suit your needs. The principal is there, but design is how you bend and break, morph and form the rules to suit your needs. You know the rules. Now go forth and break them, beautifully.

CONNECTING KITCHENS TO THE LIVING SPACE + BEYOND

You may have worked out the rough zoning of your kitchen and living spaces. If not, then finessing the connections to the other spaces may help crystallize your thoughts. The location of the kitchen and how it connects to the rest of the home and the outdoors is vital. Yet equally important are the links to the ancillary kitchen spaces such as storage and preparation or secondary kitchen spaces including the larder to allow for functionality and practicality. Here are samples of some simple yet effective ways to link the kitchen and dining areas in an open-plan space, leaving options to include access to vital ancillary storage to suit your needs.

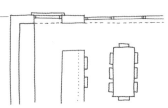

CREATE CLEAN LINES BY ALIGNING THE WORKTOP WITH THE WINDOW AND ISLAND.

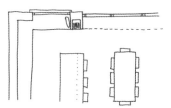

RETURN AND STEP DOWN THE WORKTOP TO MAKE A WINDOW SEAT WITH BOOKSHELVES.

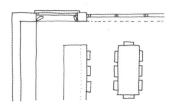

FOR A LONGER WINDOW SEAT, REDUCE THE SIZE OF THE WALL ALIGNED WITH THE ISLAND.

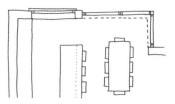

POP OUT RIGHT-ANGLED DOORS BRING LIGHT IN AND CREATE A MORE CONTAINED DINING ZONE.

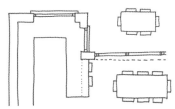

USE RIGHT-ANGLED GLAZING FOR A CONTAINED KITCHEN WITH PANORAMIC VIEWS.

Utility rooms

I imagine these ancillary spaces, the work-horse rooms that house all the muddy boots, where you wash and dry clothes and store all the things you rarely use, are like little satellites orbiting around until they are carefully worked into the design. In the 1950s and 1960s, when washing machines became commonplace in domestic life, they were generally installed where there was a spare bit of space and, most importantly, access to drainage and water. In most cases this was in the kitchen. Strangely, Nanny and Pop, my paternal grandparents, had their washing machine proudly installed in their terrazzo-tiled entrance hall, underneath a large print of a wistful looking woman with a gorgeously painted grey silk dress. Today, that entrance hall probably wouldn't look out of place in the pages of a high-fashion interiors magazine.

If we break the association of washing machines with kitchens, it frees up the utility space to be located where it is most convenient. Think back to the lines drawn on your existing floor plan and see how and where you take a pile of washing. For the majority of us, it is from the bedroom to the kitchen, and potentially then through a door into a utility room. Why do we always follow this long and tedious route? Is it just because we are so used to it?

Positioning the place where clothes and bedding are washed and dried closer to the place where they are

thrown off and stripped seems logical to me. Moving the utility room or washing machine cupboard closer to the bedrooms is a highly controversial, love it or hate it idea, probably due to noise, vibration and the potential for leaks. However, raising the washing machine up on its own plinth to decouple it from the floor and walls helps reduce vibration to a tolerable level. 'Decoupling' sounds like a new dating show, but in fact it is the fancy name for not having one rigid structure connected to another. For example, if your washer or dryer is mounted on a timber-framed plinth, then the machine itself will be placed on thick rubber feet or a mat to separate the hard base from the hard surface of the plinth. In addition, the structure itself must sit on a thick rubber mat or strips of rubber, so the vibration of the

machine gets lost as it's transferred through the rubber matting. I know this utility room chat is pretty invigorating, but bear with me. The walls themselves can be double-lined with sound deadening and fire-resistant plasterboard, which also cuts down on the ambient noise.

As with everything in life, there are pros and cons to this. Moving your utility area away from the bosom of the kitchen is not immune to this. Often, the kitchen has outside access, so getting to the washing line for energy-free dying is altered. If this is your argument, as valid as it is, how often does your washing go out on the line? And would adding a little distance to that journey be a huge pain for the benefit of not having the constant journey up and down stairs with the laundry basket anyway?

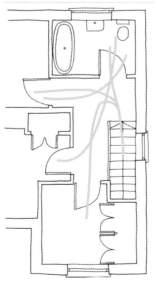

ORIGINAL LAYOUT

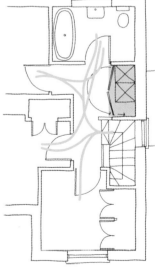

PROPOSED LAYOUT

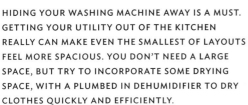

HIDING YOUR WASHING MACHINE AWAY IS A MUST. GETTING YOUR UTILITY OUT OF THE KITCHEN REALLY CAN MAKE EVEN THE SMALLEST OF LAYOUTS FEEL MORE SPACIOUS. YOU DON'T NEED A LARGE SPACE, BUT TRY TO INCORPORATE SOME DRYING SPACE, WITH A PLUMBED IN DEHUMIDIFIER TO DRY CLOTHES QUICKLY AND EFFICIENTLY.

TURNING THE TOP AND BOTTOM OF THE STAIRCASE CREATES ADDITIONAL USABLE SPACE UNDER THE STAIR AND ON THE FIRST FLOOR. THIS SPACE, FORGED SEEMINGLY OUT OF THIN AIR, IS THE PERFECT SITE FOR A UTILITY CUPBOARD. IT IS CLOSE TO THE EXISTING DRAINAGE AND AGAINST AN OUTSIDE WALL TO REDUCE NOISE.

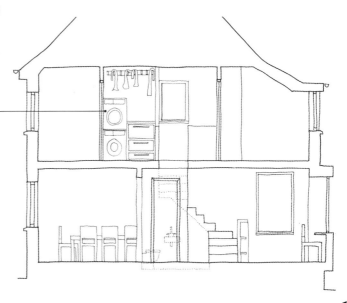

Back door

Having a 'dirty entrance' as it were into your home, in addition to your main front door, is quite a luxury. I've always known it as the 'back door', but I quite like the term 'mud room' and the picture it conjures in my mind. I see a mud room as panelled space, with dark stained-oak benches, a stag head or two, tweed jackets hanging from pegs, Wellington boots with a stylish splash of mud and maybe a dog asleep on a Persian rug. But the reality is, the back entrance usually consists of a couple of overloaded hooks that you have to squeeze past in order to get to the washing machine or dog bowl. But we can always dream.

Where there is the possibility of more than one entrance to your home, either a back or a side door or through a garage or rear porch, working this into your overall plan is just as important as your front entrance. Your design process must follow the reality of your life. If you have a back door and rarely use it, is that because of the distance from the start or your house or flat? Or maybe it has awkward or limited access? Is it hard to get to due to mobility issues or family logistics? If access isn't the issue, is the back door blocked by a free-standing fridge freezer or much needed extra storage? It is important to realize that if you have never used an access before, it doesn't automatically mean you are going to use it now even if you design it in. We are, indeed, creatures of habit.

If a secondary entrance to your home is currently failing, changing the position might work well. Perhaps look for an existing window where you can potentially just drop the windowsill to form a cost-effective door opening. If you can locate it close to either an existing toilet or your existing soil vent pipe, you can then add a WC close to the back door space. You might have even designed in a mud room. If it is your only alternative loo other than your family bathroom, then consider access from a guest's point of view, as well as how to get to it when running in from the garden or just after a walk. Your back or side door may be your main day-to-day access, therefore a pared back version of the **FLOW, LIGHT** and **STORAGE** rules work well to ensure that you still feel welcomed into your home, no matter if you are rain-soaked, carrying a buggy, child and shopping.

Tip

If your kitchen and back door are adjacent, linking any kitchen storage or larder to your mud room can be a great way to take your shopping directly to where it will be unloaded, rather than the usual method of putting everything on the kitchen work top or in the middle of the floor. Then access to the kitchen, maybe through a Narnia door (see page 137), gives a back entrance into the kitchen too.

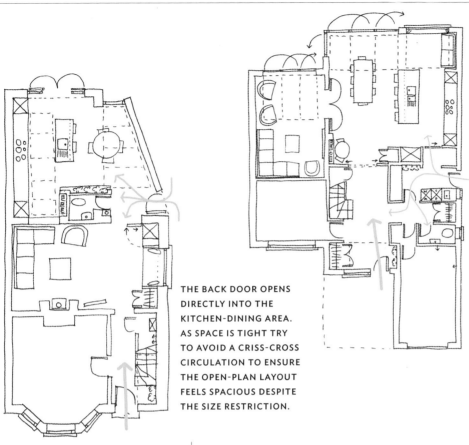

THE BACK DOOR OPENS
DIRECTLY INTO THE
KITCHEN-DINING AREA.
AS SPACE IS TIGHT TRY
TO AVOID A CRISS-CROSS
CIRCULATION TO ENSURE
THE OPEN-PLAN LAYOUT
FEELS SPACIOUS DESPITE
THE SIZE RESTRICTION.

AT FIRST GLANCE THE
BACK DOOR OPENS
INTO AN AWKWARDLY
SHAPED AND FAR FROM
IDEAL UTILITY ROOM.
BUT IN REALITY USING
THESE SPACES TO CREATE
SIMPLICITY AND CLEAN
LINES IN THE MAIN
PARTS OF THE HOUSE
CAN RESOLVE A
DIFFICULT LAYOUT.

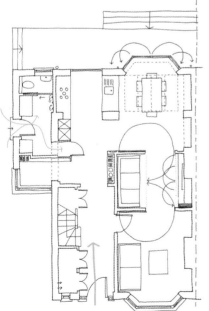

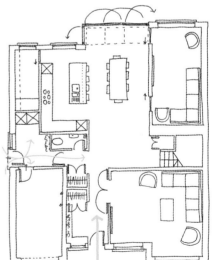

THE BACK DOOR OPENS
INTO A UTILITY ROOM
SET BACK FROM THE
COAT STORAGE AREA.
IT ALLOWS ACCESS
THROUGH TO THE WC
AND MAIN SPACE.

A NARNIA CUPBOARD
OPENS FROM THE KITCHEN
INTO THE LARDER,
UTILITY SPACE, WC AND
BACK DOOR. CONCRETE
FLOORS PREVENTED
THE MOVEMENT OF THE
EXISTING DRAINAGE,
AND SO WORKING
AROUND THESE FIXED
POINTS WAS KEY.

135

Kitchens, islands, larders + utility spaces

Until fairly recently if you asked someone to describe their dream kitchen, no doubt it would always be prefaced with the ubiquitous 'large kitchen island'. The ideal image of a show kitchen bathed in cold bright white LED light, a myriad of high gloss, glass and stainless-steel fills me with dread. Fortunately we have become slightly more sensitive to our needs within the kitchen, not simply to its outward appearance as a culinary status symbol. Now it is all about the larder. A walk-in larder or a breakfast cupboard, with practical space and storage, is currently the height of sophistication in the kitchen of dreams.

The terms 'larder' and 'pantry' both originate from French words *lardon* meaning bacon and *pain* meaning bread, were used for rooms that stored perishables and meat, dry food and bread respectively within the

kitchens of large houses. Up until the early 1900s, it was commonplace for aristocrats and the new, burgeoning middle-class households to keep a staff of butlers, cooks, maids, valets and gardeners as a sign of respectability and status. Even if a household could scarcely afford it, at least one servant was retained as a matter of principal.

As a larder was needed to be cold to keep its contents fresh, it was usually sited on an outside wall with stone slab shelving to provide rudimentary cooling. Larders were commonplace in homes right up until the middle of the 20th century, yet in 1970 only just over half of households owned an electric refrigerator. I think it is a strange irony that these rooms, once only frequented by the household serving staff whose lives would have been brutal and utterly exhausting, is now *the* luxury, must-have item in any contemporary, high-end kitchen.

Don't get me wrong, I love them. Larders and pantries are dedicated storage spaces, steeped in history with a name deriving from French; what's not to like? Incorporating a larder or pantry in a kitchen design, no matter how small, is key to designing simplicity into a layout.

I often joke that I design a home from the utility room outward. Although that is a bit of an exaggeration, I don't consider a dedicated utility space a luxury, it is an absolute necessity. The 2010 English Housing Survey reported that on average, under 10 per cent of homes have a utility room that is separate from the kitchen. I would like to change that.

THE LARDER + PANTRY

Aren't walls brilliant? Where width is no object, setting the back wall or your galley- or island-type kitchen forward by 1200 mm (47.2 in.) will give you an accessible space behind your kitchen that is ideal for a larder, pantry or even a utility room.

Narnia cupboards are storage cupboards or larders set behind standard-looking full-height kitchen doors. Incorporating a Narnia larder into a C- or L-shaped kitchen layout is ideal as they have floor-to-ceiling doors that you can use. Also, sliding pocket doors at the end of galley- or island-type kitchens are a great way to hide the working space behind without ruining the look of the kitchen. Integrated appliances give a sleek look and ensure that electrical spurs are labelled within cupboards rather than on the walls.

TO HELP RETAIN THE SLEEK CONTEMPORARY LOOK, THIS ELEGANT, SIMPLE KITCHEN HAS HARD-WORKING STORAGE HIDDEN BEHIND SLIDING POCKET DOORS, INCLUDING A LARDER, BACK DOOR AND UTILITY SPACES.

The sleeping areas

Bedrooms and bathrooms are the main domain of the private part of the house. Separating the public and private areas of a home in which there is no staircase always poses a series of design challenges. Doors and corridors have been the age-old solution, but I want to steer away from them and keep the flow and spine of circulation working within the design.

When the bedrooms are in close proximity to the living room, kitchen and dining area, visual separation is essential. Otherwise you may feel that you are stepping out of your bedroom and into a living room that is hosting a rowdy get-together when all you want to do is to get to the bathroom.

As always, it goes back to how do you use the space. How do you wake up and get going in the morning? What do you see? If you are having an early night and your partner or friend is having a party in the living room and your bedroom door opens directly into the living area, I would stay hidden in bed, quietly hoping for the reintroduction of the bed pan.

How do we create privacy where it is tricky to do so, such as in a bungalow or a flat? What are the architectural tricks we can employ to give that feeling of separation? By using the dividing methods in the previous chapters, a feeling of privacy can be created the moment you arrive at your bedroom door. You need a visual threshold that separates your bedroom from the hustle and bustle of day-to-day life. I always love hotels where the bedroom doors are set slightly back from the main corridor, either by clever lighting or being physically set back to enhance that feeling of excited anticipation. Budget hotels, on the other hand, just have rows of identical doors off a skinny corridor. This is the polar opposite of the sense of arrival we want to create in our homes, no matter how subtle.

A GORGEOUS OPEN-PLAN BEDROOM WITH AN ENSUITE BATHROOM. THE SHOWER IS TUCKED AWAY BEHIND THE BEDROOM TO MINIMIZE STEAMING UP.

Bedrooms + bathrooms

Traditionally, doors to all rooms open inward. This Victorian modesty standard was designed to allow the occupants of the room to stop what they were doing before being spied by the incomer. I like to open doors and imagine what I am able to see in the room. Can you see out of a window or are you bumping into the edge of a wardrobe? Can you see the full length of the room or are you having to sidestep around the bottom of the bed? It's not just the view from the front door – how you open any door is important.

A standard double bed is 2000 mm (78.8 in.) long and between 1200 mm (47.2 in.) wide for a small double up to nearly 2000 mm (47.8 in.) for a super king. It is standard to have at least 600 mm (23.6 in.) around the sides of the bed so you can just shimmy around, but if you can increase this to 800 mm (31.4 in.) or 1000 mm (39.3 in.) the access will be much easier, and allow for any mobility or access issues you may want to accommodate. Therefore, the minimum space around the bed is 2600 mm (102.3 in.) long by 2400 mm (94.4 in.) wide for a small bed and a whopping 3000 mm (118 in.) long by 4000 mm (157.4 in.) wide for a super king size with enough

Tip

Wardrobes set against or into the walls between bedrooms are a great space saver. You can stagger the storage between the two rooms with one wardrobe serving one room, and a second opening onto the adjacent bedroom. They don't need to be built-in wardrobes, you can simply create a space for a wardrobe you already have, whether it is an inexpensive yet handy one or a precious heirloom.

space to party, dance around and feel a real sense of space. The minimum dimensions must ideally be preserved without a door opening into the sacred space around the bed, or a wardrobe pinching a bit of the floor area.

Going back to the aspect of your home, think about where the sun rises and sets and the opportunities for views out. Many homes have the bathrooms and main drainage at the back of the building. Therefore, if you want to add an ensuite bath or shower room, it automatically goes at the back of the house, and as a result the sleeping part is thrust to the front. I can't tell you the number of times I've seen a home where an ensuite shower room with frosted windows has been squeezed in and occupies the sunniest spot with the most lovely views just because the drainage was already there. Don't get me wrong, drainage is a fixed point that needs to be worked with and not against. But rather than the lazy placement of a standard ensuite bathroom around a soil vent pipe, look at different ways to fit an ensuite bathroom into your plan. Using different shapes, sizes and configurations may allow you to keep an open aspect from your bedroom to your view or to natural light.

Designing in elements such as wardrobes and seating areas for desk space, somewhere to put on your make-up or to listen to music, can turn an average bedroom into a well-designed one without increasing the size. Carving small sections from different rooms can make all the difference, especially if you have a bigger than necessary bathroom or bedroom, stair or hallway for example. The key to the design may not lie in the bedroom itself, but in the staircase. Unlocking space by turning the stair can open up many possibilities.

I LOVE A FLAMBOYANT BATHROOM, AND VARNISHED GOLD LEAF IS A GREAT AND DURABLE SURFACE IN A STEAMY BATHROOM. STEER YOURSELF AWAY FROM BEIGE, GREY AND WHITE, AND YOUR SHOWER ROOM, CLOAKROOM OR EVEN A FAMILY BATHROOM CAN BE A PLACE OF REAL DESIGN EXPRESSION.

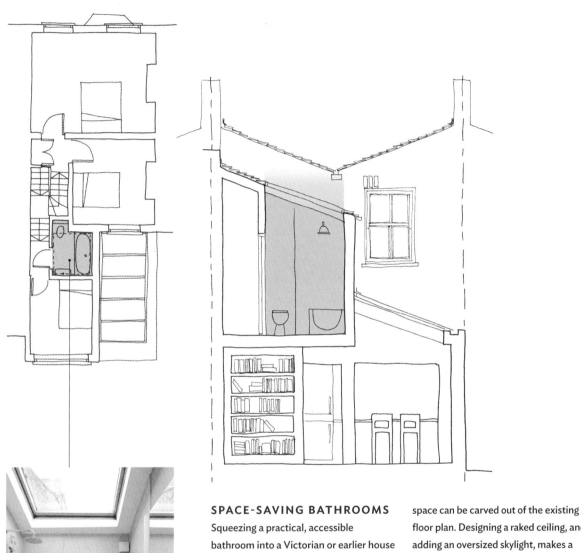

SPACE-SAVING BATHROOMS

Squeezing a practical, accessible bathroom into a Victorian or earlier house can be tricky as bathing provision was not usually part of homes built at that time. Drainage is sometimes to the rear where there may have been an outhouse, or set deep in the L-shaped floor plan prevalent in houses at the time. Installing a bathroom close to the bedrooms, without loosing one of them, is a challenge. By rationalizing the staircase, and splitting the back bedroom, a small bathroom space can be carved out of the existing floor plan. Designing a raked ceiling, and adding an oversized skylight, makes a small bathroom feel airy and spacious. Where this is not possible, and the small back bedroom becomes the bathroom, using the first 1200 mm (47.2 in.) of the room as a utility space means it is not too large, no space is wasted and the utility is installed close to the bedrooms using the bathroom drainage. Sound deadening and proofing is key to creating a laundry room that can be used day and night.

Bathrooms, ensuites + dressing rooms

You don't need an enormous space to create an ensuite bath or shower room or a dressing room. Although the smallest square shower tray you can buy is 700 x 700 mm (27.5 x 27.5 in.), you can keep that narrow width but increase the length to give a feeling of size. With a smaller space, using a wet room finish rather than an enclosed shower will help you to use the floor area more efficiently and will feel more comfortable, rather than having to squeeze in behind a shower door. Walk-through wardrobes are a space-efficient way to create clothes storage and provide a buffer between your bedroom and ensuite bathroom.

Turning your bath so that it dictates the width of your bathroom, rather than it sitting perpendicular to the entrance, enhances the feeling of width. Shorter, deeper freestanding baths at 150 mm (5.9 in.) long are a great way to achieve bathing luxury in a tight space.

A SMALLER CLOAKROOM BASIN CAN BECOME A FEATURE OF THE SPACE. WHERE POSSIBLE, ENSURE THAT WHEN YOU OPEN THE DOOR YOU ARE NOT LOOKING DIRECTLY AT THE TOILET. IF THIS ISN'T POSSIBLE DUE TO THE LOCATION OF THE DRAINS, CREATE A FEATURE TO DRAW YOUR EYE AWAY AND CHOOSE A SCULPTURAL LOO.

A STEEL-FRAMED WINDOW IS THE FOCUS OF THIS BATHROOM WITH ITS LARGE WALK-IN SHOWER AND FREE-STANDING BATH. WHEN I'M RELAXING IN THE TUB I LOVE BEING BY A WINDOW. 'MAGIC' BLINDS ARE BETTER THAN FROSTED GLASS OR OBSCURE GLAZING. THEY HAVE PIN APERTURES THAT ALLOW VIEWS OUT AND LIGHT TO FLOOD IN BUT OBSCURE ANY VIEWS FROM THE OUTSIDE IN.

INTEGRATE STORAGE

Integrating wardrobe space, drawers, shelving and possibly a place to sit or work into a bedroom layout maximizes the space because they will not be squeezed into a rectangular or square box afterward. Similarly in bathrooms, hidden storage for everyday needs such as a healthy stock of toilet rolls and cleaning products will make life so much easier. Integrated shelves in showers and next to a bath give a bespoke look. A secure shelf to hold a tablet means you can catch up on your favourite show whilst luxuriating in the tub.

HOTEL SUITE CHIC

I always find hotel visits are a great source of bedroom and bathroom inspiration. Unless you are staying in the presidential suite, they are often space-efficient and combine flow, light and storage in a compact, elegant way. Think about your bedroom as a hotel suite. Even the smallest walk-in wardrobe or long, slim ensuite shower room can feel like luxury in your own home.

VIEW FROM THE LOO

Think about the visual link between your ensuite bath or shower room and bedroom. What do you see when you open the door to each room? What do you want to look at when you wake up? Often ensuites are at the back of a building as that is where the drainage is. But there is often a view over a garden too. Look for ways to retain that view and allow light in, such as taking a slice out of the room to squeeze in a long, slim ensuite shower room. If you have the space to retain access around the bottom of the bed you could put it behind your bed.

THE BATHTUB IS THE FEATURE OF THIS LARGE ENSUITE BATHROOM AND DRESSING ROOM. SEPARATING THE WC AND SHOWER CREATES PRIVACY AND ALLOWS THE LARGE DOUBLE DOORS TO OPEN TO THE BEDROOM WITHOUT SEEING THE TOILET.

A SHOWER INSET SHELF FORMS NEAT, SEAMLESS STORAGE AND YOU CAN ADD AN EXTRA DIMENSION WITH WATERPROOF, LED LIGHTING STRIPS. AN INFRARED MIRROR WILL HEAT THE SPACE WITHOUT MISTING UP EVEN IN THE STEAMIEST BATHROOM. BE SURE YOU INCLUDE AN ELECTRICITY POINT.

Maximizing your space

Creating a feeling of space requires the coming together of form and function; beauty and practicality. Impossibly complicated layouts, lack of flow and bottle necks can make even large houses and flats feel restrictive. It's amazing how quickly a huge living room will feel tiny once you start criss-crossing it with circulation. Increasing your space is not just about adding floor area by extending it. And in a lot of cases it is not possible to physically add floor space, for example if your place is rented or there is no garden, your building is listed or has already been extended to the maximum allowed by planning regulations.

Over the years I have worked out and developed some fabulous ways that will help transform your home by creating space – or the *feeling* of space – and maximizing the areas in your home you need the most.

I love working with small spaces. For me, it provides one of the biggest challenges. Most people live with others prior to finding their own home, whether it is with family or friends, in shared houses or student accommodation, where your own space is at a premium. Growing up I was always rearranging my bedroom furniture. As the youngest, I got the smallest bedroom, naturally. There was a tiny under-eaves cupboard that I converted into my very own witch's cave – being a witch was my ultimate ambition at the time, and still is, to be fair. In my memory, this cave was enormous and I had the space to create a cauldron (made from paper), have a roaring fire (also paper) and a shelf of spell books (made from cardboard). A few years ago, I found a photo of my old bedroom, and there I was, lying on my front with only room in the tiny under-eaves cupboard for my face and hands. My witch's cave was not quite as cavernous as I remember. It's strange how our perception of space can change. When you are on-site in the middle of a build it's common for the proposed layout on the slab to seem huge. Then, when the block or stud walls start going up, it feels tiny. When boarded out and plastered the room might feel a bit enclosed but then, just like magic, once the paint has dried the rooms feel perfectly proportioned again. That is, if it has been thoughtfully designed in the first place. It is really important to know your space and understand your plans so that you will retain your faith in them even when you are feeling a bit nervous during construction, which always happens at some point.

I am a very untidy person, so I live for storage. I think the two go hand-in-hand. At home I am happiest when my husband's sock drawer is full and the kitchen work top is gleaming. I do understand the irony that I sound like an oppressed, repressed 1950s housewife, which is the polar opposite to the way I live my life. After many years of worrying, I have come to the realization that spending two full days cleaning my home if my mum is within a 20-mile radius is about shame. Shame of being what I am. Untidy. Really untidy. Please don't get me wrong, I don't iron anything or starch collars, I am a strictly utilitarian utility room user, but having a wardrobe full of clean clothes and a lovely clear kitchen signals that I am winning the battle with my own personal chaos, even just for a day or an afternoon. That is enough for me and, I hope, will be enough for you too.

Talk of utility rooms and storage might be enough to send any self-confessed home obsessive to sleep, but getting this right is the key to a happy home. Whether it is getting all the washing off the radiators by creating a utility cupboard, or having a quiet secure space for home working, it all starts with the plan. Larders, utility rooms, storage – all my favourite things in one chapter.

Rule of three:

I like to have a simple set of rules when trying to explain and establish how to get the best out of your home. Just like **FLOW**, **LIGHT** and **STORAGE**, when it is impossible to physically extend your home, another design methodology is required:

Circulation
Unused space
Pop outs

By using this system, we will be able to squeeze everything we can from your existing layout to ensure that every millimetre of space works efficiently and beautifully. Applying these design principals, we can start putting together everything we have learned to start to create your dream home with confidence.

AREAS CAN BE ZONED BY LIGHT AND CHANGES IN CEILING HEIGHT WITHIN A BROKEN PLAN DESIGN.

Circulation

I want to repeat the method from the previous chapters here, focusing now on maximizing your existing space. When I start a design and am looking over a plan with fresh eyes, the first thing I look at is how you move around the existing layout, and where the obvious areas of dead space lie. An easy way to see this on your own plans, is by using a marker pen to draw in big thick lines, your usual routes around the home. Draw how you get from the front door through to the kitchen, the kitchen through to the dining space, the living room to the bottom of the stairs (if you have them).

This technique will quickly show how you walk around day-to-day and will highlight the congested, high-traffic areas and also any unused spaces within your floor plan. More often than not, your drawn-on circulation lines will resemble a plate of spaghetti, with common routes cutting across your living and dining spaces or through your main kitchen preparation area.

Crucially, you will start to see little islands of space where there are no pen lines whatsoever. These areas are usually cut off by an intersecting route

and therefore rendered essentially unusable. Such dead, wasted spaces are critical in adding usable floor area, especially in flats or apartment blocks where physically adding square footage by extending is not an option. Space is at a premium and the magic here lies in how we bring these wasted areas into use, through rationalizing, minimizing or even eliminating circulation in the proposed scheme.

By analyzing the way your routes criss-cross back and forth, you will quickly see where the dead spaces and excess circulation are in your existing plans. You may even be surprised when you add up all the wasted space in your existing layout and get that back into usable floor area, it can be the equivalent of adding on a small extension.

Utilizing dead space

MULTIFUNCTIONALITY + PRACTICALITY

The need for multifunctional space has never been so pressing, and you could argue that the dining table has become THE most multifunctional area in the home. On the flipside, as one activity generally requires clearing away before the next one begins, then I would question its true multifunctionality. For me, to define a surface or space as truly multifunctional there should be minimal fuss and irritation attached to it, otherwise it just doesn't work that well.

We seem to share a common mindset that bigger is better when it comes to extending; that the larger the floor area the more useful the newly plastered extension will be. However, that is not always the case. I am often shown drawings with a big square extension with no illustration of how the space will come together and be used. It is surprisingly tricky to fit an elegant kitchen and dining space into a box where all of the crucial elements have been ignored. Where will the boiler go? Is there room for a utility cupboard? Where will the storage fit? How do you access the garden? These questions cannot be afterthoughts, they are a crucial part of the initial design process. The feeling of space in your home is not necessarily determined by the physical square footage, but more by the overall flow.

Whether you are in a spacious detached house or a compact urban flat, the same feeling will arise as a result: a cramped and dysfunctional home. Strikingly similar issues arise with both large open-plan and small spaces, there is often no easy way to organize how you live or no obvious, comfortable way to arrange seating and a dining area, for example. This comes down to a lack of clear zoning.

You can convert wasted areas and excess circulation into pockets of usable space using simple techniques such as turning the bottom of your stairs or moving a doorway. Decreasing the length or altering the route of excess circulation can create little pockets of usable space or even much-needed storage. Areas that were once a cramped and used as a thoroughfare or a bit of a dumping ground can be put to good use. With stairs, they are often a straight run flowing down to the front door. If you replace the bottom four or five steps with a simple winder, you will land perpendicular to your entrance door, therefore creating a niche for coats, shoes and even a seat at what was the bottom of the staircase.

LIGHT + FLOW

Pockets of light, artificial or natural, can be introduced from the side and above, illuminating different zones such as a gallery wall, a seating nook or a staircase, to give a layering effect as you look down your circulation spine.

THE INDIVIDUAL ROOMS IN THE ORIGINAL LAYOUT FELT CRAMPED AND DARK AND THE CIRCULATION CUT THROUGH EACH SPACE. MOVING THE FRONT DOOR CREATED A NEW, EXTENDED ENTRANCE HALL FILLED WITH LIGHT AND WHICH GIVES CLEAR FLOW TO THE NOW USABLE ZONES IN THE HOME.

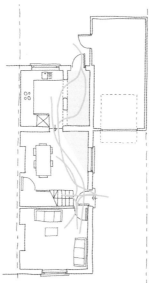

ORIGINAL LAYOUT

FINAL LAYOUT

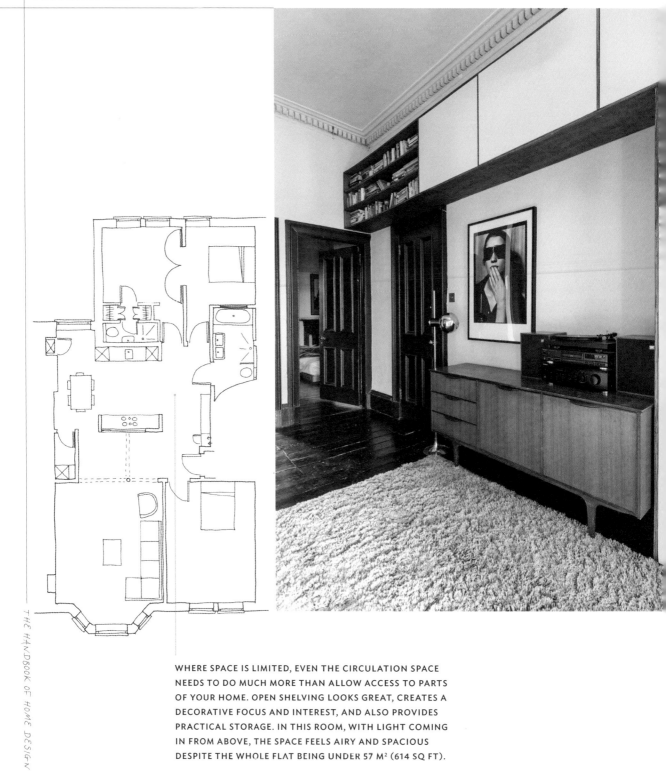

WHERE SPACE IS LIMITED, EVEN THE CIRCULATION SPACE
NEEDS TO DO MUCH MORE THAN ALLOW ACCESS TO PARTS
OF YOUR HOME. OPEN SHELVING LOOKS GREAT, CREATES A
DECORATIVE FOCUS AND INTEREST, AND ALSO PROVIDES
PRACTICAL STORAGE. IN THIS ROOM, WITH LIGHT COMING
IN FROM ABOVE, THE SPACE FEELS AIRY AND SPACIOUS
DESPITE THE WHOLE FLAT BEING UNDER 57 M² (614 SQ FT).

Framing
a view

To really help to bring your small-space design to fruition, I am going to expand on the process of creating views discussed in previous chapters. Where possible, opening up a longitudinal view through the full length of your layout immediately lifts the flow of the home and your design. Whether the view is uninterrupted, or through an opening, this simple, space-efficient spine of circulation allows light, a sense of orientation and a feeling of movement. Framing these snapshot views is a great way to create an airy spacious feel no matter how restricted your floor plan is – even if there are no external views to be had.

Cross-views also give great opportunities to create drama. When sketching your proposed designs, take a walk along your circulation route

in your mind and imagine what you are looking at each step of the way. If you have stairs, picture what you are looking at when you reach the bottom or top step. A simple winder turn to the initial or last of the final four or five treads will not interrupt the main staircase and the existing staircase itself can often be modified without being replaced, keeping costs under £1,000 ($1,156). The view as you walk down the stairs or along the circulation route can become really interesting architecturally. Think about what you can see at the moment. When you come in through the front door are you looking at a blank wall or a toilet door? Likewise with a staircase, more often than not you are confronted with your front door or a pile of jackets and shoes. Think about what you would like to

look at. Notice that I am discussing this from your point of view, not a visitor's. I think we have been sold a false narrative about the importance of show homes, show kitchens and even the concept of 'house shame'. Obviously, there are an extraordinary number of homes that don't fulfil our own day-to-day needs, or support and enhance family life let alone serve as a fantastic hub for entertaining guests on a sunny weekend. The very reason I am writing this book is to address that huge, depressing gap between the homes that we all deserve and the dismal reality of our housing stock. It is your home and your joy that I want to evoke, everyone else's will follow.

CREATING VIEWS GIVES A WONDERFUL SENSE OF DEPTH AND INTEREST, EVEN WHERE SPACE IS LIMITED. OPENING UP THE ACCESS BETWEEN ROOMS, FOCUSING ON A FEATURE – A FIREPLACE OR WINDOW FOR EXAMPLE – LINKS SPACES VISUALLY.

Unused space

Creating focus

Let's investigate the existing layout in terms of how you move around your home. On your plan, you can see the routes of circulation and how any large open areas feel when split up.

As you probably know by now, when possible, my favourite element to achieve in any home design is to have a linear view through the home as you walk through the front door. This does a number of things. It orientates you immediately, minimizes excess circulation and allows natural light deep into the plan. But how do we create that straight line of circulation on your plan?

DOUBLING-UP

Doubling-up of functions in small-space design is very different from the ordeal of clearing away books and laptops before you can lay the table, or having to hot desk with your cat. With that in mind, your circulation isn't just how you get from A to B, it must be integral to your design and enhance the function of your home with views, light and, of course, storage.

SIMPLICITY IS KEY

Again, creating a simple spine of circulation that the rooms and spaces in your home are accessed from is key to a successful layout. In small-space design, space-efficient circulation is absolutely fundamental. Another way to maximize the efficiency of circulation is to imagine a charm bracelet, where the chain is the route and the charms are the living and sleeping areas off it. Straight or circular, curved or staggered, your main spine provides the primary circulation, allowing you to move between the rest of the layout freely depending on your needs. But it is so much more than that. It is not about creating a dingy, dark corridor, but rather the spine of circulation frames views within the space and, when it's broken up using light and layering, forms the flow within your home.

Where it isn't possible to see out to a garden, terrace or picture window, then plan in a focus such as an oversized framed picture, mirror or a piece of furniture that you love, to give a similar feel of length, journey and interest. I fill awkward spots with a nice big palm or cheese plant. Houseplants go with any decorating scheme and seem to give so much depth to any room. One of the best things about dark-leaved plants, whose natural habitat is under large rainforest tree canopies, is that they don't like direct sunlight. Therefore, plants such as the fiddle leaf fig or the glossy leaved paper plant are the perfect way to brighten up a gloomy corner of your home. Although I am in no way a horticultural expert – I am not even that green fingered – I have always loved houseplants and have surrounded myself with them, in varying states of decay, all my life.

One of my earliest childhood memories is curling up in the bamboo egg chair that used to hang next to the most enormous *Monstera deliciosa*. This cheese plant, that my dad named 'Arthur', lived in the corner of the hall and was so huge it started growing across the ceiling and seemed to be attempting to take over the house. It was the first thing you saw when you walked into the house, and it provided huge drama and intrigue. Sadly, it grew so unsustainably large that it had to be moved on to the big repotting shed in the sky, but the impact that an oversized plant can give has never left me.

Pops of space

Imagine being able to conjure space out of thin air. That is exactly what we are going to do using pop outs. When I say *exactly*, I mean there or thereabouts. Where you are struggling for floor area or extending isn't an option, then any gain of space is crucial. We are going to look how to pop-out, up and in-between.

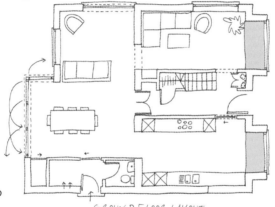

GROUND FLOOR LAYOUT

DEEP BAY WINDOWS GIVE EXTRA FLOOR AREA TO THE GROUND FLOOR KITCHEN AND SITTING ROOM, BUT CRUCIALLY, CREATE MUCH NEEDED SPACE IN THE FIRST-FLOOR BEDROOMS.

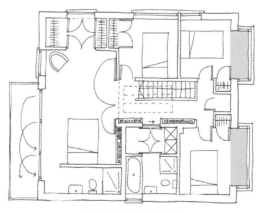

FIRST FLOOR LAYOUT

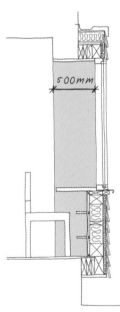

500mm

AN ORIEL WINDOW GIVES THE EXTRA FLOOR AREA CREATED BY THE POP OUT WINDOW PLUS THE DEPTH OF THE WALL. THE INCREASED DEPTH OF THE WINDOW REVEALS AND WINDOW BOARD IS PERFECT FOR SEATING OR EVEN A WORKSPACE.

Pop outs

Extending an element such as a window beyond its usual depth, which is dictated by the wall, to form an oriel window is a cost effective way to add floor area. A floor-to-ceiling oriel window, that physically extends out by less than 1000 mm (39.3 in.), will add on more once you include the depth of the wall too. They make great seating areas, window seats or even compact home offices. Rather than sitting in a cupboard, an oriel window office gives light and a view and can be tucked off a circulation space, doubling the usage.

My favourite way to give focus to your outdoor space or view is to include a picture window and integrated window seat. It is a fantastic way to create additional seating without taking up any floor space, and it is fairly straight-forward to build. You can even use an existing window and, by dropping the windowsill to approximately 500 mm (19.6 in.) from the finished floor level and increasing the depth of the window board and reveals to around 400 mm (15.7 in.), you can make a simple yet comfy place to perch. You can integrate storage, and even a bookshelf, to maximize the use of this new space. Please note that when you install glazing below 800 mm (31.4 in.), the glass has to be toughened to avoid it getting smashed by accident as it is relatively close to

the ground. Even the smallest space gain from a tiny pop out can make a huge difference. Dropping your kitchen windowsill to worktop level is another easy way to maximize light in and views out. The extra window depth provides crucial surface area that becomes ideal for growing herbs or house plants without encroaching onto your usable worktop.

WORKING WITH EXISTING FEATURES, SUCH AS A WINDOW, HELPS YOU TO FIND OPPORTUNITIES FROM WHAT MIGHT HAVE BEEN PROBLEMS. HERE A WINDOWSILL THAT IS LOWER THAN THE KITCHEN WORKTOP HAS BEEN DROPPED TO CREATE A DEEP WINDOW SEAT.

Pop ups

We often spend so much time focusing on a plan in two dimensions that we forget to look up. I am guilty of this too. At university, I was often pulled up for my lack of roof design. Fast forward many years later, and how and where the roof joins and ceiling opens up to bring light, geometry and drama into a layout is one of the first things on my mind. We seem to have become used to a design standard of flat ceiling, box-like extensions, punctuated only with a few small roof lights and a lot of spotlights. We covered design ideas and the effect of high-level glazing in Cracking common design problems (see page 50), but now I want to explore how going up can open up the possibility of creating valuable additional space.

Where you have an abundance of ceiling height, creating a mezzanine level is an effective way to increase your floor area. But how can we add extra room when we are already working in a tight, restrictive space? Broad, multipurpose areas are great, but generally they need to be fairly spacious to work effectively, and you

STAIRCASES ARE A BRILLIANT OPPORTUNITY TO INTRODUCE A DOUBLE-HEIGHT SPACE, EITHER BY INCORPORATING A MEZZANINE LEVEL OR JUST WITH A SIMPLE SKYLIGHT.

have to be able to access and use any available space in ingenious ways. This is easier said than done. For me, when working on a tight budget or in a small space, focusing on a specific function helps with the design. Whether you are short of storage or seeking a breakout area to read or relax, you can then work out how to carve just enough space from your existing layout to serve your needs. A comfortable reading or homework nook can take up little more space than a large armchair and, when designed into a staircase with built-in book shelves and upholstery, can become a practical little space as well as a real design feature as you climb the staircase.

A raked ceiling or roof glazing gives a great opportunity to create a mini mezzanine space with enough headroom to be comfortable to use. Splitting a stair after a few steps to add a landing can give a platform large enough for an office, play space or library with plenty of storage underneath the enlarged landing and easy access to the under-stair storage.

TAKING THE CEILING LEVEL UP TO THE RAFTERS CREATES A DRAMATIC ENTRANCE HALLWAY FLOODED WITH NATURAL LIGHT. THIS SIMPLE DOUBLE HEIGHT DESIGN, WHETHER A LARGE OR SMALL, CAN MAKE A STANDARD TWO-STOREY HOUSE WITH LOW CEILINGS FEEL SPACIOUS AND BRING LIGHT DEEP INTO THE CENTRE OF THE GROUND-FLOOR PLAN.

A SKYLIGHT OR HIGH-LEVEL GLAZING WILL GIVE ADDITIONAL HEADROOM TO A MEZZANINE AS GLAZING IS A MUCH THINNER STRUCTURE THAN THE FULL THICKNESS OF A ROOF.

In–between

I'm all about the space in-between. When you start to think about your rooms from floor to ceiling, visualize the space above what you are sketching in your plan drawings. In most habitable rooms, having a feeling of space above you completes it and makes the proportions feel comfortable. You wouldn't want to be sitting in your dining room with a mezzanine floor encroaching above your table. But where you are trying to steal unused space to create hard-working, space-efficient rooms, then looking up is a good place to start.

The stacking of usable space allows you to utilize void spaces above elements such as beds and even kitchen units. Bed spaces often have huge amounts of unused space above them, that can sometimes look vast in a large, proportioned room. Think about our enduring romantic notion of the four-poster bed. Historically the heavy drapes were pulled around its occupant or occupants to provide warmth and privacy, and the fabric adorning the canopy ensured no body heat was lost. Incredibly tall four-poster beds were designed and built for royalty, with obscenely and disproportionately high canopies denoting the status of the sleeper, rather than the idea of creating pleasing proportions. Today, the structure has been deconstructed to a simple geometric form, with the curtains, if any, for decoration only. I think the reason they are so popular, and so beautiful to look at, is that they make sense of the void above the bed that you don't really experience unless you are jumping up and down on it, or perhaps using the edge of your mattress to change a light bulb.

Elevating your bed so you can utilize the space underneath it is a common tactic in small space design. Alternatively, keeping the bed space lower, and the void above usable can provide a mezzanine space above for storage, a reading nook or even library depending on your ceiling height.

These voids are not always needed and when space is a premium, designing them as an integral part of the scheme allows you to make every millimetre in your home work for you and your needs.

Utilizing that in-between space with storage can be a functional way

A SIMPLE, STEEL FOUR-POSTER BED ECHOES THE GEOMETRY OF THE PANELLING ON THE WALLS. WITHOUT IT, THE BED WOULD SEEM LOST WITHIN THE HIGH CEILINGS AND TALL DOORWAYS OF THIS GEORGIAN BEDROOM.

to create interest and style. Open shelving or floor-to-ceiling doors, exposed or hidden in the design can give a feel of depth and be useful. A library wall is effectively a storage tower block, as the items are stacked vertically rather than using up floor space. Whether it is touch-latch doors that look like they are part of the wall, or panelling that opens up, it is also a great way to hide bulky gas and electricity meters, consumer units and odd bits of jutting out wall in a sleek and elegant way.

In the past, the open hearth of the cooking area was integral to the home. From the Neolithic dwellings of Skara Brae to the croft houses and tenements of the 19th century, sleeping areas were usually curtained spaces placed off the main cooking area and the hearth to benefit from the residual warmth of the fire. I adore ancient architectural techniques used by humans for millennia that are still very much in vogue today.

TAKE ADVANTAGE OF HIGH VICTORIAN CEILINGS AND BESPOKE FURNITURE TO STORE AND DISPLAY BOOKS. HERE, THE HIGH-LEVEL BOOKCASE AND CUPBOARDS ALSO FRAME THE SIDEBOARD, RECORD PLAYER AND ARTWORK BELOW. AS A RESULT THE THIN STRIP OF SPACE IN THIS HALLWAY BECOMES USABLE, PRACTICAL AND A FOCUS.

NARROW FLOATING SHELVES WITH OPEN SECTIONS DISPLAY A VARIETY OF OBJECTS AND INCORPORATE LARGER ELEMENTS SUCH AS VASES AND ARTWORK. THE SHELVES ARE A PERMANENT FIXTURE, BUT THE CONTENTS CAN BE CHANGED TO REFLECT THE HOMEOWNER'S STYLE AND NEEDS.

A CURTAINED-OFF BED NOOK IN A LARGER, OPEN-PLAN BEDROOM OR STUDIO SPACE IS AN AGE-OLD DEVICE, BUT IT'S STILL APPLICABLE IN CONTEMPORARY ARCHITECTURE. IT PROVIDES A FEELING OF WARMTH AND ENCLOSURE.

Finishes +detailing

Our homes are the places where we aspire to design and showcase the things which reflect our inspirations, personality and heritage. Creating the perfect canvas for your individual decorative flare is all in the final details. Finishes and detailing bring together everything we have discussed in this book.

We have all heard the idiom 'the devil is in the details' but you may not know the earlier version of this phrase 'God is in the details', which is attributed to one of the most influential architects of the 20th century, Ludwig Mies van der Rohe (though it was probably an old German proverb). Simply put, architects are obsessed with detail. As architecture students, we were told not to paint a material the colour that it naturally is. So never colour wood brown or steel grey. It is a rule that I try to follow, but I must admit that when it comes to deep dark grey, I love it so much that anything goes. And matt black, brass or bronze work to enhance and enrich deep inky wall tones.

When producing a mood board for your space, think about the textures that you touch and regularly use such as worktops and door handles. If you would like to create a sumptuous and moody colour palette, it is important to get the small, often-used details right, such as sockets and switches.

I am often asked how to ensure that elements in a new home design or extension, such as sliding folding doors or herringbone flooring, do not become dated. My answer is always the same. If you really love something and it works seamlessly in your space then go for it. Over the years, I have come to the realization that, like most things in life, design rules are meant to be bent and often broken. If you choose something because you absolutely adore it, not because you feel you should have it, then it will last a lifetime.

Whatever the final style you want to achieve, from sleek ultra-minimal to incredible clashing eclectic, rooting the design of your layout deep in the principals of **FLOW**, **LIGHT** and **STORAGE** will allow sightlines, sunlight and practicality to bring your home, life and style together.

THIS SIMPLE MULTIFUNCTION TABLETOP BOTH COVERS THE SNOOKER TABLE BELOW AND ALSO FLIPS OVER TO REVEAL PAINTED CHECKER SQUARES FOR BOARDGAMES TOO. PAINT EFFECTS ARE AN INEXPENSIVE WAY TO ADD YOUR OWN PERSONAL STYLE. HERE, MUTED TONES SET AGAINST COLOURFUL INDUSTRIAL SWITCHES, SOCKETS AND LIGHT FITTINGS ARE A CONTEMPORARY WAY TO GIVE A UNIQUE LOOK AND A NOD TO THE PAST.

Drawings into reality

At this stage, I anticipate that you are pleased and proud of your design concept and have a plan that you can take to an architect or technician, designer or builder so they can see a clear intention of what you want to achieve. My goal is for you to end up with a drawn concept design or two and the confidence to understand the process of design so that you are able to talk with your build team to make your plans a reality. Just as you have simplified your thoughts and ideas to get to this point, translating your scheme into physical walls, doors,

shelves and kitchen units while making sure you have an idea of the finishes and details you would like to achieve is pivotal.

Now is the time to bring out Pinterest and the magazine pages that inspire you. You may find that what you want is slightly different now. Rather than a pile of beautiful, honed interior photographs, you are looking for the individual, component parts that make the whole. Analyze the images and look for the flow, the light and the storage and how these details can be assimilated into your

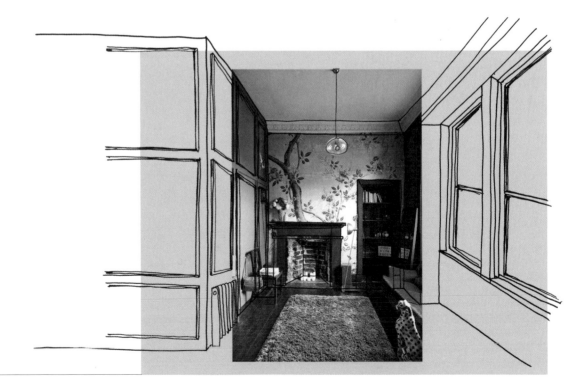

final build. If there is an image you particularly love, try to work out the age of the property and whether this interior style would suit your home. Break it down so you can identify the elements that you love and can use.

Pay close attention to the items around the home that are sometimes forgotten because they are so ubiquitous: the doors, the ceilings, the, dare I say it, grid of spotlights. Look at the lighting and where and how spaces are lit. Can you see any zoning formed within the room or rooms? What about the views through

and the layering? Using all that you have learned, you can start to work out exactly what it is that you love and bring it to your own design. Using the bones of good design, you can now start to flesh out your layout with your personal style and taste, whether that is flush fitting, contemporary doors that disappear into the wall or stripped and stained reclaimed panelled doors that make a statement. The possibilities are endless and the result will be personal.

MOOD BOARDS

As an architect, I always avoided putting a mood board together, thinking they were the preserve of interior designers. How wrong I was. I now find it such an enjoyable way to visualize how the room or whole build will come together inside and out. I often put them together way before we even get on-site, to accompany the concept plans, so you can swap and change as the project develops, yet still keep the vision of your home burning bright through the ups and downs of building or renovating.

CREATING A MOOD BOARD

Once you've defined your space, the fun of creating a mood board will not only help you form a sense of your style, but also aid your decision-making about the colours, fabrics and lights you may want to add to a scheme.

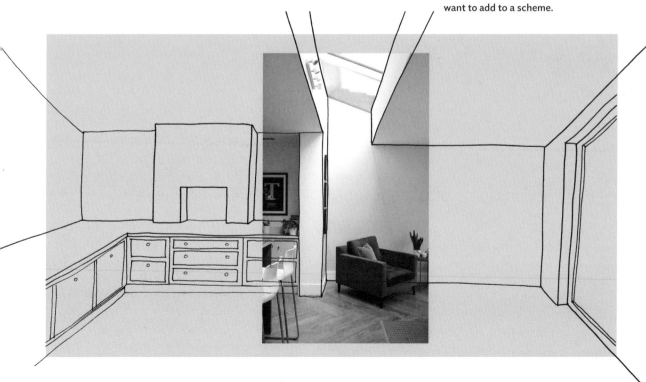

1

2

8

9   5

4

6

7

THE KITCHEN AS A ROOM IN THE HOME
EARLY GEORGIAN TOWN HOUSE

3

This kitchen can be seen from all areas of the living space. The original red plaster inspired the dark tones and so the kitchen needed to be bright and reflect light without being white and clinical. Having one dark colour for elements such as beams and shelving unites the scheme. My favourite grey – RAL 7021 – works in any scheme. With the stripped walls and bare plaster, the sleek red lacquered doors contrast completely but the warm red complements the brown in the walls and the dark floor.

1. STRIPPED-BACK BARE PLASTER
2. GLOBE LIGHT
3. DEEP MUSHROOM EGGSHELL PAINT
4. DEEP CHARCOAL SHELVING AND ACCENTS
5. ORIGINAL FLOORBOARDS, STRIPPED AND WITH A DARK STAIN
6. RECLAIMED CAST IRON COLUMN RADIATORS
7. RED LACQUERED HANDLELESS DOORS
8. SIMPLE BLACK FURNITURE
9. RECLAIMED FIRE SURROUND

BROKEN-PLAN LIVING AREA
1960s BUNGALOW

Clean lines and a unified palette of natural materials allow this living room to be a visual part of a broken-plan bungalow layout while retaining its own identity. The pink band painted on the wall follows the line of the low, kitchen dividing wall and surrounds the corner sofa to give a feeling of sunken seating and cosiness that can be lacking in open- and broken-plan spaces. A clear, matt finish enhances the beauty of the birch ply and protects it. The light grey cork floor runs through the entire space, further uniting the zones, while the natural finish contrasts with the contemporary fixtures and fittings. The floor is water resistant and absorbs sound.

1. TWO-TONE PAINT IN WHITE AND PALE GREY
2. SIMPLE BLACK, POWDER-COATED LIGHT FITTING
3. BIRCH PLY FINISHED WITH CLEAR MATT OIL
4. INTEGRATED PLANTERS ALONG THE LOW-LEVEL DIVIDING WALL
5. REPRODUCTION BAKELITE SOCKETS AND SWITCHES IN PASTEL COLOURS
6. PALE GREY CORK VENEER ENGINEERED FLOORING
7. DARK CHARCOAL CORNER SOFA
8. CONTEMPORARY COLUMN RADIATOR
9. PALE PINK MATT PAINT
10. BLACK WASHI TAPE IS USED TO CREATE PANELS AND BOXES ON THE PAINTED WALLS AND PLYWOOD

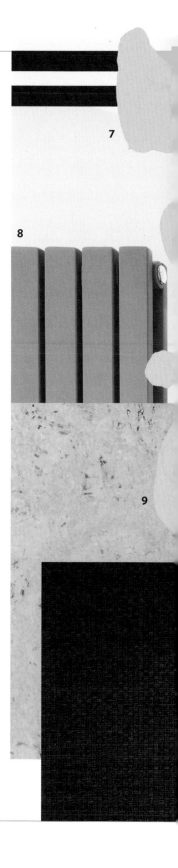

1

2

7

6

6

3

DARK TIMBER BATHROOM
LATE VICTORIAN TENEMENT FLAT WITH NO OUTSIDE ACCESS

1. **DARK-OAK STAINED BIRCH PLY WITH CLEAR MATT VARNISH**
2. **EXTERNAL RECLAIMED SHIP'S LIGHT**
3. **RECLAIMED SOLID IROKO SLATTED FLOOR**
4. **CLEAR TOUGHENED GLASS SHOWER SCREEN**
5. **DECORATIVE TOUCHES TO THE NATURALISTIC INTERIOR SCHEME**
6. **COST-EFFECTIVE SANITARYWARE**
7. **BRITISH-MADE CAST-BRASS BATH SPOUT AND TAPS**

This internal bathroom has no natural light, apart from that borrowed from a rising partition mirror used to separate the bathroom from the bedroom when closed, and to unite the two rooms when it is raised. Rather than trying to emulate a light and bright bathroom, the style is dark and intimate.

The room is tanked, almost giving a paddling pool effect between the reclaimed wooden panels and slatted floor. The iroko slats were reclaimed from a school gymnasium. The planks were cut down, sanded and oiled to bring out the remarkable grain. The wall panels are separated by 15 mm (0.6 in.) shadow gaps and a touch-latch opening to two panels creates storage. A mix of inexpensive white, square-edge sanitaryware mixed with high quality cast brassware ties the bathroom together and allows the budget to be used for items that are touched all the time. Rather than spotlights, the ship's lights feel unique without being clinical. The bonus of industrial external or shipping lights, whether reclaimed or new, is that they are waterproof. Lighting and electrics must be IP65 rated when installed near the bath or shower, or IP44 if at a safe distance.

LIGHT-FILLED LIVING ROOM
EARLY GEORGIAN TOWN HOUSE

This south-facing living room is filled with direct sunlight from late morning until early afternoon, therefore going too pale would have given a bleached look. Stripping back the walls provides a neutral yet decorative finish and a chinoiserie pattern was projected or stencilled onto the wall and painted over, to give texture and depth to the room. The off-white paint has a warmth not possible with standard white paint, and the panelled sections complement the original dado rail. The lengths of timber used to make the picture frames were bought direct from the manufacturer and create an almost perfect panel effect when fixed to the wall and painted. Dark stained floorboards create a contrast in this light-filled room. Salvage and pieces of vintage joinery with accents of gold leaf, pattern and jewel-like colours such as rich, red velvet pop against a refined palette of materials. Houseplants, especially with dark leaves, grow brilliantly in larger rooms. The darker the leaf, the more adapted the plant is to thrive in low light. They can therefore bring focus to a dark and cramped corner and work incredibly well to break up the living room.

1. BARE STRIPPED-BACK PLASTER PAINTED WITH A CHINOISERIE PATTERN
2. BRASS LIGHT BULB HOLDERS WITH A COLOURED FLEX. THE RED TIES IN WITH THE RED VELVET SOFA
3. WARM, OFF-WHITE PAINT
4. PICTURE FRAME PANEL LENGTHS, CUT AND MOUNTED
5. GOLD LEAF
6. RECLAIMED MID-20TH CENTURY SIDEBOARD
7. ZEBRA RUG
8. MID-20TH CENTURY VELVET SOFA
9. PLANTS AND CUTTINGS

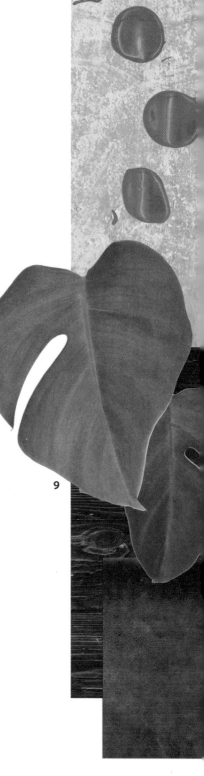

9

1

2

3

4

5

6

7

8

Case studies

Here I am going to put into practice everything I have discussed to show how I have utilized my three design rules of **FLOW**, **LIGHT** and **STORAGE**. I talk about the problems with the existing layouts, then how I combined and shifted around my three rules to create finished designs.

Using four projects, parts of which have been featured throughout this book, I bring each project together. From early Victorian through to mid-20th century, I will give a broad explanation of how to put design theory into use and show you the results.

PAINT EFFECTS ARE AN INEXPENSIVE WAY TO ADD YOUR PERSONAL STYLE IN A SPACE. MUTED TONES AGAINST COLOURFUL INDUSTRIAL SWITCHES, SOCKETS AND LIGHT FITTINGS GIVE A UNIQUE LOOK AND A NOD TO THE PAST IN A CONTEMPORARY WAY.

1960s BUNGALOW

**THREE BEDROOMS / YOUNG FAMILY /
BUDGET APPROXIMATELY £100,000 ($ 115,580)/
SOUTH-EAST OUTLOOK OVER REAR GARDEN**

Single-storey living, whether a bungalow or apartment, can present real issues in terms of getting light in and views out. When you get the design right, the flow and views can be inventive and help occupants with mobility issues.

The original layout of this Bedfordshire bungalow hadn't been hugely altered or extended since it was built, so the entrance hall, although spacious, looked directly at all the doors. It was dark with little storage, and there was no sense of orientation, no view out and no sense of where the heart of the home was. The kitchen was at the front, overlooking the driveway, had one door into the open-plan living and dining room, and no direct view or access to the rear garden.

I didn't want to make any vast structural alterations or move the existing bathroom. I used the budget to extend to the rear and introduce glazing above the entrance to give real impact. The width of the existing hall was continued to the rear to create a beautiful slice right through the home. As there were no water tanks above the entrance hall, I was able to design a glazed, double-height space that emphasized the separation of the public parts of the home from the private areas.

Views were created and framed within this entrance slice, and structure and storage hidden away inside the walls to give a feeling of broken-plan living. The kitchen and dining area look toward the garden, and the living room toward the original fireplace. The original kitchen became a snug or office space to give extra flexibility, with a utility room taken from here to take advantage of the existing kitchen drainage.

The entrance hall skylights bring light deep into the plan, and solar gains help to heat the home without overheating the sitting or living areas. The space can be easily ventilated and heat circulated when necessary.

STORAGE WALL
THE WALL THAT FORMS THE ENTRANCE HALL AND SEPARATES THE LIVING AND SLEEPING SPACES IS EXTRA DEEP TO PROVIDE CRUCIAL HIDDEN STORAGE AND A PLACE TO DISPLAY RECORDS AND TRINKETS IN THE LIVING AREA.

FLOW
THE ENTRANCE HALL GIVES A SENSE OF FLOW THAT VISUALLY SEPARATES THE BEDROOMS AND LIVING SPACES AND BRINGS NATURAL LIGHT INTO THE CENTRE OF THE PLAN.

PRIVATE + PUBLIC SPACES

THE CONCEPT BEHIND THIS DESIGN IS THE SEPARATION OF THE PRIVATE BEDROOM SPACES AND THE PUBLIC LIVING AREAS. THIS CAN BE CHALLENGING IN A SINGLE-LEVEL DWELLING.

L-SHAPED KITCHEN + ISLAND

THE SQUARE ISLAND EXTENDS THE KITCHEN LAYOUT AND INCREASES STORAGE CAPACITY. THE BIRCH PLY FINISH UNIFIES THE BROKEN-PLAN LIVING SPACE.

ORIGINAL FEATURES

THE NEW LIVING AREA IS IN THE SAME LOCATION AS THE PREVIOUS LAYOUT, WITH THE NEW KITCHEN IN THE EXTENSION BEYOND.

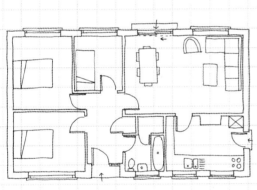

ORIGINAL LAYOUT

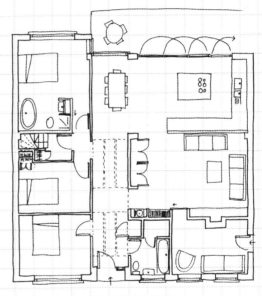

FINISHED LAYOUT

BEDROOM + ENSUITE

THE ENSUITE IS TUCKED AWAY WHEN YOU ENTER THE BEDROOM AND SO YOUR FOCUS IS ON THE BED ITSELF, AS WELL AS THE VIEW OUT TO THE PICTURE WINDOW BEYOND.

1890s VICTORIAN TENEMENT FLAT

THREE BEDROOMS / COUPLE /
BUDGET APPROXIMATELY £60,000 ($ 57,790) /
SOUTH-FACING LIVING ROOM OVERLOOKING BUSY ROAD

This south Glasgow tenement flat enjoys a large south-facing bay window; however it overlooks a motorway. The original layout was intact with a cramped bathroom, large kitchen diner and the three big cupboards with panelled doors that are common in tenement flats. The ceilings are over 3.5 m (11.5 ft) high with ornate cornicing and ceiling roses in the living room and entrance hall. The original timber sash windows had been replaced with white, now yellowed, uPVC casements. These were the first thing to go. As the owners were a young couple with no family plans, there was no need to retain all three bedrooms and I wanted to shift the layout to allow for contemporary living. To open up the layout a large proportion of the budget was used to remove the main living room wall. I also wanted to take advantage of the high ceilings to create a hidden mezzanine space. By carving space from the two rear bedrooms, I increased the size of the bathroom using the existing drainage.

A circulation with the kitchen at the heart created a flowing space and a sliding mirror opened a visual link between the living room and kitchen-dining space. A utility cupboard at the end of the living space ensures a dedicated washing and drying space. Storage was dispersed to take advantage of the high ceilings. This extra floor area created a dramatic entrance, with framed internal views and enough space for a larger dining area. The enlarged open-plan living room has a floor-to-ceiling curtain that can contain it in the winter months or for privacy. The rear bedrooms were combined to create a dressing room with walk-through wardrobe and shower.

UTILIZE SPACE
A WALK-THROUGH WARDROBE AND ENSUITE SHOWER ROOM SEPARATES THE BEDROOMS. DESPITE THE LOSS OF SPACE, THIS ROOM, WITH ITS OFF-SET FIREPLACE, FEELS WELL-PROPORTIONED.

STORAGE AS DISPLAY
ARRANGE ITEMS YOU USE REGULARLY ON OPEN SHELVING TO REDUCE THE DUSTING YOU NEED TO DO.

BATHROOM GLAMOUR
THE DARK AND MOODY
TIMBER-PANELLED
BATHROOM COMPLEMENTS
THE INTERIOR SCHEME OF
THE WHOLE FLAT. A SLIDING
MIRROR OPENS THE SPACE
TO THE BEDROOM BEYOND.

GALLEY KITCHEN
THIS IS OPEN TO
THE ENTIRE SPACE
AND THE FOCUS
OF THE LAYOUT.
IT COMPLIES WITH
FIRE REGULATIONS.
ALWAYS CHECK FOR
FIRE COMPLIANCE.

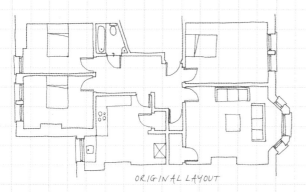

ORIGINAL LAYOUT

STORAGE
REMOVING THE ORIGINAL STORAGE
MEANT THE NEW STORAGE HAD TO
BE INTEGRATED INTO THE DESIGN.
THE HIGH CEILINGS ALLOWED FOR
THE CREATION OF HIDDEN AND
EXPOSED STORAGE SPACE THAT
FORMS A FEATURE OF THE SPACE.

FINISHED LAYOUT

ORIGINAL DETAILS
INFILLING THE OUTLINE
OF THE PREVIOUS
LAYOUT IN A
CONTRASTING
MATERIAL ALLOWS
THE SKELETON OF THE
ORIGINAL FLAT TO
BECOME A FEATURE OF
THE DESIGN.

1930s SEMI-DETACHED HOUSE

**THREE BEDROOMS / COUPLE / BUDGET
APPROXIMATELY £120,000 ($ 23,116)/
SOUTH-FACING GARDEN VIEW**

The semi-detached house built in the first half of the 20th century is a common sight. They have often been extended to the rear, resulting in a long and dark plan with large amounts of wasted space. In this Watford house, the homeowners were keen gardeners, and the large, south-facing garden was central to the design. Storage was an issue but the utility cupboard was already located upstairs. Creating a view through to give a sense of flow and light was key. It was not possible to move the front door and it was a beautiful feature of the original architecture of the home. The flow line frames the view through the house to the garden beyond. Floor-to-ceiling doors hide the existing toilet, all storage including the manifold for the new underfloor heating system, and give access out to the side of the house.

The 3 m- (10 ft-) deep extension is the perfect width for a dining space in front of the kitchen with doors to the garden for alfresco eating. The seating area opposite it is tucked back from the spine of circulation, making it a great space to relax. A slot window gives a sneak view down the length of the garden, and from the garden to the house. The lowered ceiling of the extension is joined to the main house by a dramatic, seamless slot of glazing across the entire width. This connects the lower extension without the need for a beam or bulkhead protruding from the ceiling. Views and access to the terrace and garden were crucial. The flush threshold reinforces the sense of flow, but more importantly the simple line of sight and circulation together with level access future-proofs the home in terms of usability and accessibility for years to come.

LIGHT
POCKETS OF NATURAL LIGHT FLOOD THE DIFFERENT AREAS IN THE PLAN. THE HIGH CEILINGS OF THE ORIGINAL HOUSE ARE CONNECTED BY A STRIP OF HIGH LEVEL GLAZING THAT BRINGS IN SUNLIGHT WITHOUT THE RISK OF OVERHEATING.

STORAGE
HUGE AMOUNTS OF
STORAGE, INCLUDING
COAT CUPBOARDS AND
A LARDER, ARE HIDDEN
BEHIND THE TOUCH LATCH
DOORS. THEY ALSO LEAD
TO A WC AND ACCESS TO
THE SIDE OF THE HOUSE.

REPURPOSED DINING ROOM
THE KITCHEN IS LOCATED
IN THE OLD DINING
ROOM. THIS ALLOWS THE
PROPORTIONS, CORNICING
AND FIREPLACE TO BE
RETAINED AS AN ECHO OF
THE ORIGINAL LAYOUT.

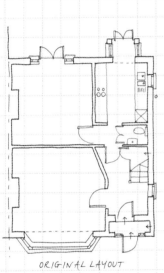

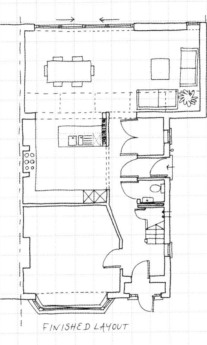

ORIGINAL LAYOUT

FINISHED LAYOUT

LOOKING OUT
THE OWNERS ARE
KEEN GARDENERS,
AND WINDOWS AND
GLAZED DOORS
FRAME THE VIEW OF
THE GARDEN FROM
THE SEATING AREA.

FLOW
THE ENTRANCE HALL AND STAIRWAY
HAVE BEEN OPENED UP TO CREATE A
VIEW THROUGH THE HOME AND GIVE
HINTS OF THE SPACES IN FRONT OF YOU.
THIS CLEAR LINE OF FLOW DIRECTS YOU
TO THE HEART OF THE HOME WITH A
FOCUS ON THE GARDEN.

EARLY VICTORIAN TERRACE

THREE BEDROOMS / FAMILY WITH OLDER CHILDREN / BUDGET APPROXIMATELY £120,000 ($ 138,695) / NORTH-FACING GARDEN

The layout of most Victorian houses is not conducive to easily adding a family bathroom when updating and modernizing. This terraced house is a classic case in point. The small, damp bathroom was located at the back of the house on the ground floor. Sometimes when these homes are renovated the bathroom is put upstairs above the kitchen which means the loss of a bedroom. Unless you don't need that bedroom, or are able to convert the loft, then this is not a favourable option. So how do you move a bathroom to the first floor without losing a bedroom? Here, the homeowners created a compact family bathroom and retained the bedroom using an oriel pop out window.

The infill extension – the alleyway between terraces has already been carried out – producing a strange kitchen layout with a discoloured plastic skylight that is now practically opaque. Bringing the kitchen into the dining room allows the chimney breast to be utilized in the design for the hob and allows ventilation through the stack. Access and views are maintained to the front room with a sliding pocket door, and the living room has more usable wall space and a feeling of containment. The new dining area in the infill extension is filled with light to compensate for the north-facing garden and the seating area opposite with a library wall hides drainage and makes a space for the children to do homework or become a sitting area. Tucked away from the slightly expanded stair line is a utility area and toilet with two doors for discretion. The ceiling of the new extended ground floor is pitched to give a feeling of height, space and drama while maintaining low eaves levels to the neighbours.

KITCHEN AS A ROOM IN THE HOME
THE KITCHEN IN AN OPEN-PLAN SPACE CAN STICK OUT LIKE A SORE THUMB. BY USING CONTRASTING, DARK TONES THE KITCHEN IN THIS LONG AND THIN HOUSE LOOKS SET BACK AND LIKE A SEPARATE ROOM.

NATURAL MATERIALS
THE MATTE, DARK TONES OF THE KITCHEN UNITS CONTRAST WITH NATURAL MATERIALS SUCH AS BRASS TO GIVE A GOLDEN GLOW THAT HIGHLIGHTS AND WARMS THE WHOLE SPACE.

FRAMING WITH GLAZING
THE BLACK STEEL DOORS
ARE THE MAIN FEATURE
FROM BOTH THE HOME
AND GARDEN. THEY
LINK AND FRAME THE
VIEWS AND THE SUBTLE,
INDUSTRIAL FEEL WORKS
WELL WITH THE RED BRICK.

ZONING WITH LIGHT
OPENING UP THE ROOF WITHIN
OPEN-PLAN SPACES CREATES
ZONES WITHOUT THE NEED FOR
PHYSICAL SEPARATION. THE ROOF
GLAZING ABOVE THE DINING
AREA FLOODS THE TABLE WITH
LIGHT AND BRINGS NATURAL
LIGHT TO THE DARK KITCHEN.

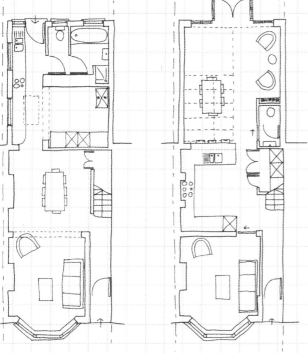

ORIGINAL LAYOUT   FINISHED LAYOUT

BATH WITH A VIEW
A BATH AT A WINDOW
CAN BE A LOVELY
ADDITION TO A HOME IF
NEIGHBOURS AREN'T A
PROBLEM. A BEDROOM
WAS REPLACED BY A
LUXURIOUS BATHROOM
WITH FREESTANDING BATH
TUB AND WALK-IN SHOWER
THAT SUITS THE SCALE OF
THE RENOVATION.

STAGGERED VIEW
WHERE A DIRECT VIEW
THROUGH FROM THE FRONT
DOOR ISN'T POSSIBLE,
RETAINING A SENSE OF FLOW
MEANS THE VIEW MUST BE
SLIGHTLY STAGGERED. YOU
CAN JUST SEE THE FRONT
DOOR FROM THE LIVING AND
DINING SPACE.

WALLS + CEILINGS

Limelite Heritage
Swains Park Industrial Estate,
Park Road, Overseal,
Derbyshire, DE12 6JT
limeliteheritage.co.uk

The Limecrete Company
Room 1, Unit 1D Langley
Trading Estate, Langley Road,
Chedgrave, NR14 6HD
limecrete.co.uk
@thelimecretecompany

Mainline Mouldings
83 Langar Industrial Estate,
Harby Road, Langar,
Nottinghamshire, NG13 9HY
mainlinemouldings.co.uk
@mainline_mouldings

William Boyle & Co
52-58 Darnley Street,
Pollokshields, Glasgow, G41 2SE
wmboyle.co.uk
@wmboyleinteriors

DOORS + WINDOWS

A J Hilston
22 Bog Road, Laurieston,
Falkirk, FK2 9PB
ajhilston.co.uk

Door Deals
Broombank Road,
Chesterfield, S41 9QJ
doordeals.co.uk
@doordeals

Mike Honour Doors and Windows
Unit 85, Northwick Business
Centre, Blockley,
Moreton-in-Marsh, GL56 9RF
mikehonourwindows.co.uk
@bespokesteelwindows

In Steel
590 Kingston Road,
London, SW20 8DN
@insteel.uk

Barnglass
7 Sandiford Road, Kimpton Road
Industrial Estate, Sutton, SM3 9RN
barnglass.co.uk
@barnglassgroupltd

Sealed Units Online
159 Princes St, Ipswich IP1 1QJ
sealedunitsonline.co.uk
@glasssealedunitsonline

Velux
Worldwide
velux.com
@velux

Velfac Windows
Worldwide
velfac.co.uk
@velfacwindows

JOINERY + FITTINGS

Häfele
Worldwide
hafele.co.uk

CT1 Adhesive and Sealant
Unit 6, Ashtree Enterprise Park,
Newry, Co Down, Northern
Ireland, BT34 1BY
ct1.com
@ct1sealant

KITCHENS

High End Kitchen
9 Marylands Road,
London, W9 2DU
highendkitchen.co.uk
@high.end.kitchen

IKEA
Worldwide
ikea.com
@ikea

ELECTRICAL FITTINGS

CDA
The CDA Group Ltd,
Harby Road, Langar,
Nottinghamshire, NG13 9HY
cda.eu
@thecdagroup

SWITCHES + SOCKETS

Swtch
Studio 2, Star Brewery,
Lewes, East Sussex, BN7 1YJ
swtch.co.uk
@swtchuk

Selectric UK
Cow Lane, Oldfield Road,
Salford, Manchester, M5 4NB
selectricuk.co.uk

UK Electrical Supplies
5A Windmill Road, Hampton
Hill, Middlesex, TW12 1RF
ukelectricalsupplies.com

LIGHTING

Enamel Shades
Unit 14 Stirchley Trading Estate,
Hazelwell Road,
Birmingham, B30 2PF
enamelshades.co.uk
@enamelshades

Coldhabour Lights
Herne Hill Road,
London, SE24 0AD
coldharbourlights.com
@coldharbour_lights

Daze Neon
Trafford Park, Manchester, M17 1SJ
dazeneon.com
@daze_neon

Prolite Lamps
Meadow Park, Bourne Road,
Essendine, Stamford, PE9 4LT
prolite-lamps.co.uk
@proliteled

National Lighting
Unit 8, Grand Union Trading
Estate, Abbey Road, Park Royal,
London, NW10 7UL
nationallighting.co.uk
@nationallightinguk

BATHROOMS + PLUMBING

Victoria Plum
victoriaplum.com

Bathrooms By Design
225-231 Lower Mortlake Road,
Richmond, TW9 2LN
bathroomsbydesign.com
@bathroomsbydesignuk

The Poured Project
128 Womersley Road,
Knottingley, WF11 0DQ
thepouredproject.com
@thepouredproject

Crosswater Bathrooms and Brassware
Lake View House, Rennie Drive,
Dartford, DA1 5FU
crosswater.co.uk
@crosswater_uk

Topps Tiles
Thorpe Way Grove Park,
Leicestershire, LE19 1SU
toppstiles.co.uk
@toppstiles

Lefroy Brooks
Worldwide
lefroybrooks.com
@lefroybrooksofficial

Wunda Underfloor Heating
Castlegate Business Park,
Caldicot, South Wales, NP26 5AD
wundatrade.co.uk
@wunda_group

Milano Radiators
bestheating.com
@bestheatinguk

FLOORS

Flooring Superstore
flooringsuperstore.com
@flooringsuperstore

Recork
Unit 3D Priory Park, Quarry Wood,
Aylesford, Kent, ME20 7PP
recork.co.uk
@recorkuk

Hempwood
301 Rockwood Road, Murray,
Kentucky, KY 42071, USA
hempwood.com
@hempwood_

V4 Wood Flooring
Greenbays Park, Carthouse Lane,
Horsell, GU21 4YP
v4woodflooring.co.uk
@v4woodflooring

Direct Wood Flooring
Henson Close, Bishop Aukland,
County Durham, Dl14 6WA
directwoodflooring.co.uk
@directwoodflooring

Composite Prime
Leeds, England
composite-prime.com
@compositeprime

FINISHES + DECORATION

Littlefairs Wood Finishing
Unit 2, Lions Drive,
Blackburn, BB1 2QS
littlefairs.shop
@littlefairswoodfinishing

Broken Hare
9 Tudor Lane, Cardiff, CF11 6AZ
brokenhare.couk
@brokenhare

Gold Leaf Supplies
Unit C, Ogmmore Court,
Abergarw Trading Estate,
Bridgend, CF32 9LW
goldleafsupplies.co.uk
@goldleafsupply

Metal Supermarkets
Worldwide
metalsupermarkets.co.uk
@metalsupermarkets

Bold and Noble
Bold & Noble, 13 The Ridgeway,
Hitchin, Hertfordshire, SG5 2BT
boldandnoble.com
@boldandnoble

The Monkey Puzzle Tree
Unity Business Centre, 26
Roundhay Road, Leeds, LS7 1AB
themonkeypuzzletree.com
@the_monkeypuzzletree

Bambino Emporium
32 Church Road,
London, SE19 2ET
@bambinovintageshop

Ben View Antiques
Unit 3 Lomond Galleries,
Alexandria,
West Dumbarton, G83 0UG
@benviewantiques

The Paint Shed
Units 8-9, 20 Munro Road,
Stirling, FK7 7UU
thepaintshed.com
@thepaintshedcompany

Anaglypta
Retford Wallcoverings,
Coringham Road Industrial
Estate, Gainsborough,
Lincolnshire, DN21 1QB
anaglypta.co.uk
@anaglyptauk

Graham & Brown
grahamandbrown.com
@grahamandbrown

Dulux Heritage
duluxdecoratorcentre.co.uk/
heritage
@duluxheritage

This Modern Life
13c Marlborough Park,
Harpenden, AL5 1DZ
thismodernlife.co.uk
@thismodernlife

Surface View
268 Elgar Road South,
Reading, RG2 0BT
surfaceview.co.uk
@surfaceview

Rebel Walls
Worldwide
rebelwalls.com
@rebelwalls

Curtains2go
Worldwide
curtains-2go.co.uk

Diedodoa
5a East Preston Street,
Edinburgh, EH8 9QQ
diedododa.com
@diedododa

Immortal Botanica
141 Stanley Road,
London, TW11 8UF
cassandraking.co.uk
@immortalbotanica_
cassandraking

Paraphernalia Vintage
8 King Street, Margate
and 2 Addinton Street,
Ramsgate, Kent
@parahernaliavintage

Hunter Stoves
Trevilla Park, Slaughterbridge,
Cornwall, PL32 9TT
hunterstoves.co.uk
@hunterstovesgroup

French Connection Homeware
Worldwide
frenchconnection.com
@frenchconnection

Our Lovely Goods
Worldwide
ourlovelygoods.com
@ourlovelygoods

TOOLS + SUPPLIES

Festool
Worldwide
@festool

Thornbridge Timber Merchants
Thornbridge Yard, Lauriston
Road, Grangemouth, FK3 8XX
thornbridgesawmills.co.uk
@thornbridgesawmills

Cut Tec Cutting Technologies
Zenith Park, Whaley Road,
Barnsley, S75 1HT
cut-tec.co.uk

Häfele Ironmongery
Worldwide
hafele.com
@hafele_international

Evolution Power Tools
Longacre Clost, Holbrook,
Sheffield, S20 3FR
evolutionpowertools.com
@evolutionpowertools_uk

George Boyd Hardware
25 Loanbank Quadrant,
Glasgow, G51 3HZ
george-boyd.co.uk
@georgeboyduk

ADDITIONAL PICTURE CREDITS

GAP INTERIORS/DOUGLAS GIBB 111BR,
FIONA WALKER-ARNOTT - DESIGNER
NICOLA HOLDEN 133L, JULIEN
FERNANDEZ 70, MARK ASHBEE 133R,
NADIA MACKENZIE 111BL, VERONICA
RODRIGUEZ 71; INTERIOR ARCHIVE/
MONTSE GARRIGA/DESIGNERS MARIA
LLADO AND CARINA CASANOVAS
67R; ISTOCK/ONURDONGEL 102;
SHUTTERSTOCK/DRIMAFILM 22AB,
LEON WILHELM 12; UNSPLASH/TIM
MOSSHOLDER 18;

Acknowledgements

When the literary agent, Silé Edwards, contacted me two years ago asking "Have you ever thought about writing a book?" I responded immediately with a two-thousand-word manuscript and a firm "YES." In the preceding few months, I had been devising and shaping the way I approach home design to form a tangible guide to give insight and help shed light on how an architect works.

Thank you Silé for all the help, encouragement and time you gave me, reading my work in those early stages and giving me the confidence that I lacked. You got the sense of fun and lightness that I wanted to bring to this book and brought me together with Joanna Copestick and Samhita Foria at Kyle Books and also the inimitable, incredible, Helen Bratby. Helen, thank you for your warmth, enthusiasm, endless zoom meetings and brutal honesty, bringing such style and panache to my words and pictures, and the laughter we had doing it. Thank you to the wonderous James Balston and husband Jochen, your styling and photography of my projects and patience with me and my untidiness, has made this book. And thank you to Matt Gillies, who dropped everything to come to draw me for the front cover of the book. It was a dream to work with you all.

It feels like a lifetime ago when I started as a student in the Mackintosh School of Architecture with dreams and ambitions, but not a clue what I was getting myself into. Thank you for the unwavering support of my amazing parents, especially my fathers shed building prowess. The help, encouragement and DIY skills of my sister's Kate and Helen and their wonderful husbands' Brian and Dave have been invaluable and oft called upon. Thank you also to Linda, Des and Alison for being the best in-laws a person could ever ask for.

I would have never of thought that when I set up on my own in 2008, cutting my teeth on small extensions and loft conversions, that there would be a day where there was a place for my ideas and this book. Thank you so much to Jude Tugman, co-founder of Architect Your Home, where I started, whose concept of the "initial consultation" has changed the face of domestic architecture.

Thank you, Fiona Murray, one of the strongest women I know. You single handily got me through the final day of getting the Crystal Palace Underground Toilet flat photo ready, when I could hardly see for crying. The time, effort and beautiful photography you gave me from start to finish on that project was the catalyst for where I am today.

To my best friends Matt, Kumud and Gulfam who have always had more faith in my abilities than I do, and made me know my worth. Thank you to wonderful Colin Nwadike of New Wave Academy, whose kindness and encouragement made me feel like I could achieve anything in both mixed martial arts and indeed, life. To the author and my dear friend, James Brooke-Smith, thank you for the time you dedicated to proofreading my very first ever writing, without wincing.

Thank you to Kitty Walsh and Joff Wilson of Remarkable Television, and especially Joff for putting up with and taming my endless, loathsome self-doubt while filming *Your Home Made Perfect*.

To Rebecca Galbraith, one of the most talented architects and tutors I know. Bringing focus and pride to small-scale, residential architecture in your university course is the start of the change in our profession. Thank you to all the Siren Sisters and the incredible Kate Watson-Smyth for your enthusiasm, encouragement and support. You are some of the greatest women in the industry, I am proud to know you all and call you my friends.

Thank you so much Claire, Jo and Erin from Unhooked Communications. Your joyous and infectious energy and ability to listen to me ramble on about this book from day one, has been an inspiration. (..and yes, I'm still waiting on the *Strictly* call...)

And thank you to Chris Fitton, without your time and expertise I probably wouldn't be writing this book. A big thank you also to Russell from Glen Coe, you and your USB cable saved the day that weekend.

Most importantly, I can't begin to express my gratitude and love for my husband, Kevin. Writing and finishing this book, our builds and renovations, the brilliant ideas and epic fails are all a joint effort with you, emotionally and physically. I couldn't do any of it without you. Thank you.

And finally, to my daughter Zuzu, your laugher and smile brings sunshine into our lives, every single day.

An Hachette UK Company
www.hachette.co.uk

First published in Great Britain in 2023 by
Kyle Books, an imprint of Octopus Publishing Group Limited
Carmelite House
50 Victoria Embankment
London EC4Y 0DZ
www.kylebooks.co.uk

ISBN: 9781914239267

Distributed in the US by Hachette Book Group,
1290 Avenue of the Americas, 4th and 5th Floors, New York, NY 10104

Distributed in Canada by Canadian Manda Group,
664 Annette St., Toronto, Ontario, Canada M6S 2C8

Publisher: Joanna Copestick
Project Editor: Samhita Foria
Design: Helen Bratby
Photography: James Balston*
Production: Caroline Alberti

Printed and bound in China

10 9 8 7 6 5 4 3 2 1

additional photography credits: please see page 190